MAKE A SUCCESS
OF FAMILY LIFE

Other Books in the Need2Know Series

A full list of books can be obtained from
Need2Know, 1-2 Wainman Road, Woodston, Peterborough PE2 7BU

Help Yourself to a Job
Step by step into work
Jackie Lewis

Buying a House
Ease the path to your new front door
John Docker

Stretch your Money
Get more for your £££'s
Michael Herschell

Make the Most of Retirement
Live your new life to the full
Mike Mogano

Make the Most of Being a Carer
A practical guide to lightening the load
Ann Whitfield

Breaking Up
Live your new life to the full
Chris West

Successful Writing
The beginner's guide to selling your work
Teresa McCuaig

Superwoman
A practical guide for working mothers
Marion Jayawardene

Work for Yourself and Win
A practical guide to successful
self-employment
Ian Gretton

The Expatriate Experience
A practical guide to successful relocation
Bobby Meyer

Forget the Fear of Food
A positive approach to healthy eating
Dr Christine Fenn Accredited Nutritionist

You and your Tenancy
A helpful guide to feeling at home
Sue Dyson

Improving your Lifestyle
Live a more satisfying life
Mike Mogano

Safe as Houses
Security and safety in the home
Gordon Wells

The World's Your Oyster
Education and training for adults
Polly Bird

Everything you Need2Know About Sex
The A-Z Guide to Increase your Knowledge
Anne Johnson

Travel Without Tears
An Essential Guide to Happy Family
Holidays
Marion Jayawardene

Prime Time Mothers
A Positive Approach to Delayed Maternity
Lyn Cartner

Parenting Teenagers
Make the Most of this Unique Relationship
Polly Bird

Planning Your Wedding
A Step by Step Guide to the Happy Day
Niamh O'Kiersey

Forthcoming books

Coping With Bereavement
Julie Armstrong-Colton

The Facts About the Menopause
Coping Before, During and After
Elliot Philipp

Get What You Pay For
A Guide to Consumer Rights
Gordon Wells

Take a Career Break
Bringing Up Children Without Giving Up
Your Future
Astrid Stevens

© Michael Herschell 1996
ISBN 1 86144 020 0
First published by Need2Know, 1-2 Wainman Road,
Woodston, Peterborough, Cambridgeshire PE2 7BU
Tel 01733 390801 Fax 01733 230751

Edited by Kerrie Pateman
Design by Spencer Hart
Typesetting by Forward Press Ltd

MAKE A SUCCESS OF FAMILY LIFE

A Guide to Getting Along

Michael Herschell

Need2Know

Acknowledgements

I would like to thank my family and friends for their advice and comments. In particular, I would like to acknowledge the valuable help provided by my wife Sue, Ludlow Police Crime Prevention Department, the members of Homestart in Ludlow, The Telford Muslim Trust, The Sikh Missionary Society, Baldeep Hungin, Jenny Morris and the many contributions from readers of The Christian Herald (most of whom prefer to remain anonymous).

The material presented here represents the findings and opinions of the author and not necessarily those of any other agency. The information given is that which applied in the summer of 1996. Some addresses, telephone numbers or other details may have since changed.

If you find any errors or omissions please let the publisher know for inclusion in future editions.

Michael Herschell

Contents

Introduction

Introduction

Q: *What is a family?*

You may think a family is the traditional 2.4 children living with their two parents. And yes, this is a family but it is only one of many types. Look around you and you will see single parent families, step families, a couple with no children, a household of several generations and even a single person whose parents, uncles and aunts, brothers and sisters live in other towns. All are families or part of another family.

In a nutshell, a family is any social group that shares the same house or activity. In the wider sense, a school, class, office or football team can each be seen as a sort of family. However, for the purposes of this book, the term 'family' is used in a more narrow sense to refer to people who share the same house, the same parents or children and who share matters such as income and spending.

Q: *What is a family for?*

A family can have many functions. At the root of the family is our need as human beings to live with other people. We need people for company and for care.

Since time began, people have grouped together for these reasons. The family group in ancient times would most likely have been a large household made up of several generations of blood relatives as well as servants and slaves. It was here that the children, sick and elderly could be cared for in a protected environment. Adult members would be responsible for supplying the family with food and household items as well as for the training and education of their young folk. And at the end of the twentieth century, these functions still apply.

The family is where children obtain their values, where they learn to love and where they learn their responsibilities to the family and to the world outside. It is where we can balance our individuality with our dependence on relationships with others. It is where we can share our hopes, our happiness, our anger and our love.

This is not to say that things have to stay the way they were done by our parents and grandparents. We live in changing times and the family needs to adapt and change with them. The most successful families are those that remain flexible to the new possibilities around them: the changing roles of both women and men; the increasing recognition of the contributions that can be made by grandparents and by people with disabilities. Ultimately, the successful family will also be the one that is actively involved as a family in the wider community.

We all have a family of some sort whether we like it or not and this book is therefore for everyone. It is aimed at showing you how to get on with the other members of your family from the newly born baby to the elderly great grandmother who leaves her teeth on the sink at bedtime.

Hopefully you are reading this because you want to improve your own family life, whether it be how you bring up your children or how you can actively involve your elderly relatives.

It will take you through some of the basics in bringing

up children, look at how to deal with crises, discipline, coping with a career, change and relationship problems. Finally, it will give you some tips on how to enjoy your family and how to get on with everyone by looking at things through their eyes.

Questionnaires

Try these simple exercises before you go any further. They will help you focus your mind on family matters and on what you hope to get out of reading this book.

There are no 'right' and 'wrong' answers. These surveys are merely to get you thinking and perhaps talking with your family.

Stresses & Strains

What do you feel are the main pressures on you as a parent? Tick one box for each question.

	Never	Occasionally	Frequently	Always
Too much responsibility				
Not enough help from others				
Money troubles				
Partner away too much				
Demands from work				
Grandparents' interference				
Unsuitable house				
Lack of nearby facilities				
Disagreements with partner				
Other.............................				

A Good Parent?

Which of these statements about parental qualities do you feel apply to you?

	A little	A lot
I am understanding and patient		
I am reasonably well organised		
I am a good listener		
I am actively involved with my family		
I make realistic demands on		
a) my partner		
b) my children		
I am generous		
I have firm standards for behaviour		
I am fair		
I am flexible		
I praise and encourage my family		
I give my time freely to my family		
I respect a) my partner		
b) my children		
I enjoy being a parent		
I think I am a good parent		
My family think I am a good parent		
Other...		

Who Does What?

Who performs all the tasks involved in running a family? If you do 70% or more put 'M'; If your partner does

70% or more put 'P'; if you share the task by both doing between 30% and 70% put 'S'.

Earn the family income	
Cooking	
Cleaning	
Washing and ironing	
DIY jobs and repairs	
Shopping	
Gardening	
Looking after the children	
Make decisions	
Discipline the children	
Other.............................	

Does everyone do a fair share? Which tasks do you wish you had more help with? Which do you like doing? Which do you hate?

Now you are focused on your family matters, and ready to take the steps towards a successful family life.

A World of Families

Before we get down to the nitty gritty of family life in Britain at the end of the Twentieth Century, it is worth taking a few minutes to look at the world of families around us. In every country and region of the world, the family unit is at the centre of organised society.

Its importance is recognised from Aborigines to Zulus. All the major tasks of living from childcare to providing food and shelter, are shared out between the family members.

The major world religions emphasise the central importance of the family and much of their writings set out recipes for a successful family. Whilst it is not intended here to promote any one of these religions, there is a lot that can be learned from them whatever your own particular beliefs may or may not be.

Hindu

It is common to find several generations living together in a Hindu family. In the vast majority of families, the women cook for everyone and the men earn the money needed by the family. How this money is spent is decided by the older members of the family who take into account everybody's needs.

It is always a family duty to care and support its elderly, sick, disabled or poor members.

The relationship between parents and children is notable in that it is based upon mutual respect towards each other. The parents provide the necessary shelter, food, education, money and care for both young and old. In return, the children show respect and obedience to their parents by studying hard and by avoiding selfish actions that might reflect badly on the family. The oldest son is also made responsible for the actions of his younger brothers and sisters.

To sum up, a Hindu family works well because it is each member's duty to make sure that the rights of the others are protected.

Sikh

As with Hindus, children in a Sikh family are taught to accept the rules laid down by their parents as well as to trust their wisdom. Sikh parents see it as their duty to provide a setting in which the children can gain values and learn to live with others.

The Sikh family always tries to sort out the problems its members have whether it be divorce or debt. Any family that cannot solve its difficulties is seen as a bad family.

One Sikh mother discovered how extra special her family was by the support it gave her after the trauma of a divorce. She writes, '*They created and provided a cohesive family atmosphere for my son so that he grows up to value and respect the family unit.*' (B.Hungin) Their help with child minding, financial matters and mediation have allowed her to continue with her career as well as encouraging her to face up to the world.

Muslim

At the heart of the Muslim family is the requirement to take care of its old people including, if necessary, aunts and uncles. Age definitely comes first and children are brought up to be respectful, considerate and tolerant of the older members of the family. Children are taught never to interrupt or argue with them nor to make them believe they have become a burden to the family.

All children are treated equally and fairly though discipline can often be strict. Parents are encouraged not to be over-protective and not to be disappointed if their children do not come up to expectations. Muslims believe that parents should set a good example so that their children grow to be kind, independent and willing to help others.

Much emphasis is put on mothers who are seen to be 'responsible for the nurturing of the next generation' and for promoting a 'caring Islamic society'. For these reasons Muslim women are encouraged to put their family before a career for the family system 'nourishes human unselfishness, generosity and love.' (Telford Muslim Trust)

Jew

Judaism teaches parents and children to have mutual respect for each other and that each have certain responsibilities towards the other. Parents are expected to feed, clothe and educate their children as well as ensure they can support themselves when they are grown up. One of the Jewish books of teaching, the Talmud, says, 'Teach your son a trade or you teach him to become a robber'. They are also expected to teach them survival skills such as swimming and road safety and, above all, to give moral guidance through example.

Children, on the other hand, are expected to take care of their parents. This includes being tactful and not pointing out their shortcomings, not hurting their feelings and not giving them cause for irritation.

The commandment 'Honour your father and mother' is a duty that works both ways. Parents have to make themselves the kind of people their children will want to respect.

The weekly Sabbath is of great benefit in holding the family together. It focuses on home life with the whole family being together for a celebration meal the evening before. In the morning they all go to the synagogue and then spend the rest of the day relaxing together, playing games and visiting relatives.

Christian

Children are seen as a gift from God. For this reason parents are expected to treat their children properly and to ensure their rights are protected.

The Christian family depends upon each member to play a part in the family through mutual service. There is a need for unselfishness and self sacrifice from all members if the family is to live happily together.

Love for others must be given freely and with no thought of seeking anything in return. This is particularly relevant when it comes to attitudes to the elderly members of the family. While it may no longer be possible to care for old people within the family home, it is still important to make sure they are personally looked after.

What people say

From the many letters received, the same points are mentioned time and time again. Here are some of them:

- ✿ 'The Family that prays together stays together.'
- ✿ 'It is very important for the whole family to sit together and talk things over.'
- ✿ 'Children over 12 should be treated as friends rather than children.'
- ✿ 'A successful family life depends upon communication, understanding, listening, sharing,...willingness to compromise.' (Nirmal Singh)
- ✿ 'Just be nice and helpful...work hard at school.' (teenage step-child)
- ✿ 'It helps to have lots of help from friends and family.' (Mrs S.Hughes)
- ✿ 'Stay relaxed and laid back...look at any problems as if they were somebody else's.'
- ✿ 'Listen to your children and give them one to one time. Let them discuss important family issues as a family so they feel that they are involved.' (D.Eyre)
- ✿ 'Remember that you were once a kid yourself...try and stay young at heart...don't get too serious.'
- ✿ 'We try to get on with each other most of the time. We also have time on our own with our own interests.' (Shelley)

✿   'Have lots of fun with the children and give them lots of love and attention - not just when they demand it.' (Mrs T.Baker)

From this whistle stop tour, several common elements have emerged. By putting them together, you can see that a successful family will be based on the following pointers:

✿   All members of the family are important and each has his or her part to play

✿   There should be mutual respect between the generations within the family. To be of value this respect has to be earned

✿   It is everyone's duty to look after the others

✿   It is important to have regular times when the family is together for relaxation and to provide an opportunity to sort out problems

✿   There should be tolerance, consideration and tactfulness between family members

✿   Have fun together!

2

Starting a Family

The thought of becoming a parent for the first time can be more frightening than the idea of bungee jumping from the top of a crane. Probably your greatest fears will include such questions as: how will I cope with a new born baby, will I be able to balance the child's needs with mine and, most of all, will I get it right?

There is no single correct way to bring up children but whichever way you choose, it has to be based on love, care, fairness and flexibility. That last word is important because a child's needs change rapidly throughout his or her childhood and you will have to be flexible to cope. What worked for a two year old won't necessarily work for a six year old.

This chapter will take you through the main stages in a child's development and give you some hints on ways you can cope.

Needs

At birth babies are 100% dependent upon their parents for the provision of all their needs. By the time they have grown up and reached adulthood, they are likely to be almost 100% independent and able to cope with providing everything they need for themselves.

This is not to say that there is a cut off date or age when you as the parents can say, 'Right that's it, your time is up, you've had all you're ever going to get from me. Goodbye.'

Hopefully, if you've been a reasonable parent, neither you nor your children will ever want to completely part company. Think for a moment of your own parents. Even now as an adult of 25, 35 or 45, you still need your parents' support, affection, unconditional love and approval just as they will need the same from you. If you don't get it the feeling of rejection can be just as devastating at 44 as at 14.

Children need many things from their parents beginning at the most basic level with food, warmth and shelter. You, as a parent will be providing an environment in the family home that meets these essential demands throughout their time living with you. The array of other needs you will also be meeting include:

✿ All aspects of physical care
✿ A place of safety and harmony
✿ Unconditional love through physical affection, respect, praise

and friendship as well as through consistency, patience, tolerance and the giving up of your time
- ✿ Stimulation and encouragement that allows them to develop their own potential and skills
- ✿ Discipline as you guide them towards becoming responsible for their own actions and the part they play in the home and in the wider community

Whatever your children's ages, your role as a 'good' parent will continually require you to meet these needs. However, at different stages in their development there will be special requirements that you will need to consider.

The first twelve months

From the very beginning, babies primarily learn through their senses - touch, taste, hearing, smelling and vision. As they become more aware of the environment around them you must ensure it is sufficiently stimulating by providing a variety of fabrics and toys to touch and taste; kind and friendly voices, music, rattles and bells to listen to; scents to smell; mobiles, coloured shapes and patterns to look at.

Try to bring your baby into the centre of family activity as much as possible as she/he will enjoy watching what is going on. Take her/him around with you but be careful not to leave the baby alone in the room with other small children.

Soon, they will become more active and they will want to move their eyes, hands, feet and head. You can provide stimulation by surrounding them with toys that make a noise when grasped, toys to reach out for and things that are clean and safe for them to put in the mouth.

By the end of the first year you can expect to see your baby crawling about and making his/her first tentative efforts to stand up and walk. You should be aiming to provide them with activities that encourage them to try out, explore and move. They will want a safe space to move in and stable furniture (or knees) to pull themselves up on. They will particularly enjoy rhymes that combine physical contact and movement with music such as 'Round and round the garden like a teddy bear...'

Toddlers

From around 18 months onward, your child will be walking after a fashion. You are on the threshold of that stage marked by periods of frantic energy as the toddler happily rushes around looking into everything, touching everything and making a noise. Then, the next moment you find a tearful or sleepy child on your hands that needs comfort and quiet. Toddlers may be prone to accidents as they will not have developed a sense of danger so extra care must be taken at all times to ensure their environment is safe.

Here, you will be looking to provide items to pull and push such as an empty cardboard box on a string, a pram, a fabric bag to fill, empty and generally drag around, baby walkers and so on. Toddlers enjoy being able to climb, dress up, play with toys that develop their manipulating abilities and a host of other stimulating activities. The most important thing you can provide, however, is yourself - a lap to sit in, arms to hug and comfort, a body to play games with and a voice for discussion, singing and talking.

Early Childhood: 2 to 6 years old

By the time the novelty of having a baby around the

house has worn off, many parents make the mistake of only seeing their job as to train their child for adulthood. How many times have you heard someone address their five year old as 'young man' or 'young lady'? How often have you heard a six year old being told to grow up and act his age?

Childhood is not just a preparation for future adulthood, it's a special part of life to be valued for itself. So, yes, you will be guiding the relative newcomer to the world through the pains, joys and pitfalls of life but this must not be at the exclusion of an enjoyment of the moment. Splashing in puddles is just as valuable an experience as learning the alphabet.

Through the next few years, the key points are:
- ✿ To build on what your child can already do
- ✿ To meet all of your child's needs - physical, health, mental and spiritual

From toddling to the first year in school, children are continually widening their experiences and exploring all aspects of their environment and themselves. Bit by bit, with a little help from their adult family friends, they are transforming into responsive human beings. Your aim is to encourage them to gradually find their place within life and society. For this they will need time to be by themselves in which they can go over and extend what they have recently learnt and they will need activities they can organise and direct themselves.

By now you should be involved in one of the many support groups set up to help parents and children. Involvement in a parent/toddler group, playgroup or nursery has numerous advantages ranging from the opportunity for you both to mix with a wider circle of adults and children to having somewhere to share and discuss your own experiences and problems as a parent.

The transition from home to community is an important stage in your child's development and it will go more smoothly if you also attend the group. Both you and your child will pick up stories, songs and activities to take back home with you.

Middle Childhood: 6 to 12 years old

Once your child is safely ensconced in their first or primary school, don't think your responsibilities are at an end - far from it. As your children stretch their wings to explore the wider world, they need to know there is a secure and predictable home to come back to.

This period is emotionally a quiet one when compared with the ups and downs of early childhood and with the turmoil still to come during adolescence. This is the time when they are most eager to learn about the world around them and consequently are especially receptive to teaching both at school and in the home.

You will, of course, continue to provide the haven of comfort, security, patience and approval as before. But this is the time to be unstinting in the provision of opportunities for learning. Whatever happens at school , you are still the most important people when it comes to promoting your children's learning. It is important to discuss what goes on in school and to take a genuine interest in your children's achievements - they will thrive on your interest and praise. In addition, they need constructive toys; a wide variety of both fiction and non-fiction books; trips to museums, galleries, shows and concerts. Finally, basic life skills such as cooking, mending, cleaning and making things are still areas of learning that are best achieved in the home.

Adolescence: 12 to 17 years old

This is a period of great change for your children and is also the time when there is likely to be the most conflict with you, their parents. Physical changes with the onset of puberty will result in a growth spurt and an increasing awareness of themselves as individual sexual beings. Coupled with this will be an increase in emotions as adolescents become more self-aware, self-critical but also increasingly less confident and less sure of themselves.

As parents, you really do have to be ready to ride out a storm, for you are likely to be first in line when it comes to any sort of emotional outburst. But there is no guarantee when it will come or, in fact, if it will happen at all. Many children pass through adolescence with barely a whimper and without even realising it has happened.

During this transition from child to young adult, your child will be renegotiating their relationship with you. Whereas before they had readily accepted your rules with respect and obedience, now they are going to want a relationship that is both more equal and mutually trusting. They will constantly want to move the goal posts on how they are treated with regard to coming home times, spending money and responsibilities.

Hopefully, if you already have a relationship built on mutual trust and care for one another, these conflicts can be resolved through 'sensible' discussions. But when there is a more violent outburst, the onus is on you to make the first move towards reconciliation. Throughout this period of anxiety, unhappiness, turmoil and sometimes delinquent behaviour, you still need to provide a caring, reliable environment.

3

The Working Parent

It's hard enough bringing up children as a full time occupation. But when you are also holding down a full time career or a part time job, the task of holding a family together can often appear to be almost impossible. How you manage will largely depend upon many factors such as the co-operation you receive from your partner and the ages of your children.

It is important for you, your partner and your children to recognise that both parts of your life - your family and your career - have their place. There are going to be times when your family will have to come first. For example, you may need time off work at short notice to care for a sick member of your family. It's therefore just as vital that your employer recognises that these times are going to occur. It may be most inconvenient to your job but when the time comes your family needs must always take precedence.

Having said all this does not mean that your career can never come first. Your family must equally recognise that there will be times when you have to work late, go away for a meeting, study for an extra qualification or work extra hours for colleagues who have to take time off for their family needs.

The problem comes when both your family and your career need to come first at the same time. What do you do when there's an important meeting to attend and your youngest is home from school with sickness and diar-rhoea? This is when you are going to need a contingency plan. Whilst you must always hope for the best you must also prepare for the worst.

Career or Family: contingency plans

✿ Prepare for your absence from work. Whenever possible, keep colleagues informed of what you are doing. When an important event looms at work for which you are principally responsible, get your main ideas down on paper. Then, should you be absent on the big day, someone else can fill in for you as well as put forward the ideas you have been working on

✿ Consider holding smaller internal meetings in your house. If you have to stay home to look after someone, arrange for everyone to come to you. That way, you can be on hand if an emergency arises

✿ Find at least two different sources of child minder that you can call on in an emergency. These people should be known and trusted by your children so that they won't be too alarmed if they are there to look after them rather than you. Always consider members of your own family first such as aunts, uncles, your parents, adult brothers and sisters - and not forgetting your own partner. Next in line could be a neighbour or close friend. It always helps to establish ground rules for things like payment and available times before you need to contact them

Everyday Strategies for the Working Parent

Apart from knowing how to deal with emergency situations, it is worth considering the everyday management of your home and career. Most of the time this will simply be a matter of establishing manageable routines. But if you don't establish these right from the start you could end up being the family doormat. As with all routines, they shouldn't be too rigid and they must allow for the natural development of the children and changing needs of the family members.

- ✿ Division of labour. Make sure everybody does their fair share. It's not fair if you come home from a long day at work and find the rest of the family lolling about on the sofa in front of the television waiting for you to get their tea. If everyone in the family works long hours, you could perhaps construct a rota so that all those who can, take a turn at cooking the evening meal. Make it a rule that whoever cooks the meal doesn't have to clear up and wash up afterwards

- ✿ Look at the regular household tasks and when they need to be done. Ideally, you should aim to get the majority of chores done at the weekend. Prepare meals such as casseroles and pies in advance. An all out attack on cleaning, changing beds, washing and ironing by the whole family can get everything done within a couple of hours. Organise your shopping by keeping a communal list of items to buy

- ✿ Learn to Delegate. Rotas are all very well but if someone is totally incapable and completely reluctant, then it is a waste of time expecting good results. In this case, tinker with the rota to allocate jobs according to ability, expertise and willingness. Of course, you will have to be careful that this doesn't give someone the chance to get all the cushy jobs and get out of the less pleasant ones.

  When you delegate a job, it's important to really leave them to get on with it. There's nothing worse than having someone standing behind you telling you what to do every two seconds and criticising each stage of your efforts. Delegation means just that - you need someone to do a valued task for you because you haven't the time or the energy to do it yourself. It also means that you trust them to do it adequately. After all, they can always be told where to find you if they need a bit of extra advice

✿ Learn to say 'no'. Your family and your employer must know that there are limits to what you can be asked or expected to do. If demand exceeds your time and energy, point out that if you do one thing you won't be able to do the other. Ask them to prioritise what they want you to do

✿ With an employer, you may have to tread more carefully as a blunt refusal could backfire on you. There is no hard and fast rule on when to say no with an employer so it will be down to your judgment. During a busy period at work, it may be that all employees are expected to put in extra hours. On the other hand, if you're asked at very short notice and you already have an important appointment involving your family, you could justifiably ask to be excused. Generally speaking, employers are worth cultivating whenever possible. By showing your willingness to change your plans and take on extra jobs, your employer may be more amenable to you needing time off to take your child to the doctor

✿ Look out for Signs of Stress. You should keep an eye open for this within yourself and also within other members of the family. When you see this happening it is important to act early. Stress usually shows itself in a number of ways that slowly come to light over a period of several days or weeks. It normally indicates that you are overdoing it. Some of the more common tell tale signs include: being irritable with everyone, being fidgety, always having to be busy doing something, regularly disturbed sleep, frequent headaches and other minor ailments

✿ Learn to Relax. Even when you aren't showing obvious signs of stress, you should try to build regular periods of relaxation into your life. Relaxing activities should be a complete contrast to whatever task you are taking a break from. If you've spent four hours in front of a word processor, a suitable activity will be one that stretches you physically - a walk, a swim or a manual task in the garden. On the other hand, if you've just spent three hours vacuuming the house, making the beds and hand washing half a dozen woollens, then a sit down in front of the television may be the most appropriate thing to do

✪ Develop a hobby and make sure you allocate regular times to pursue it

✪ Take proper rest breaks at work and at home. Go away from your immediate workplace by moving into another room or going outside

✪ Get up ten minutes earlier than you have to each morning. This gives you time to potter around at leisure instead of rushing around like a wild thing with your eye permanently fixed to your watch

✪ Share your problems with someone else - your partner, a friend, a work colleague or even your line manager

✪ Stay calm. Pace yourself and take your time over tasks even when you're in a desperate hurry - you'll make fewer mistakes and you'll probably get the job done just as quickly

✪ Learn a suitable relaxation technique. This must be something that works for you and which you enjoy. It might be a regular swim, walking the dog, skipping, meditation, yoga or simply finding a quiet spot in which to have forty winks

A Special Word for Fathers

Everything in this book is aimed at whoever is managing a family - whether it be as mother, father, aunt, uncle or step-parent. Where there are two parents running the family I treat both as equals and do not try to dish out household tasks as being the particular responsibility of the male or female parent.

However, this goes against the bulk of public opinion which still tends to see mothers at home bringing up the children and father as the breadwinner who stays late at the office and who only comes home to discipline the children or pay the bills. Unfortunately, this stereotype concept is ingrained in most walks of life. The male worker is expected to work long hours whereas it is assumed that the female will work shorter hours because of her family commitments. Maternity leave is universally acceptable but paternity leave is rare and frequently frowned upon. Few stores have 'parent and baby' rooms for changing and so on.

For many men, being a father is a role that is kept private - workplace nearly always takes precedence over the family. Similarly, much of the conflict between mother and father revolves around the division of domestic tasks. The mother wishes that her male partner would do more, yet there appears to be no flexibility at work to allow him to do this.

So what can you do?

✷   At work, make it clear from the start that your family is important. Talk to your employer and insist that you are treated with the same flexible attitude as your female counterparts when it comes to family priorities and emergencies

✷   At home, become involved in your family from the very beginning and show that you want to play an equal role in bringing up the children. They haven't displaced you and they are not competitors for your partner's affection

✷   Discuss the problems that cause friction between you - that you need half an hour or so doing nothing when you first come home from work; that you don't work long hours from choice but because it is expected of you; that you shouldn't be depicted as the bogeyman who will 'discipline' the children when you get home

☼ When both of you work, try to arrange your periods at work so that you can both develop a career and yet be fully involved in the parenting role

☼ Make sure you find time for your family but also to be alone with your partner

☼ To the outside world, show that you are proud to be a parent which is, after all probably the most important job you'll ever do

☼ Being a good father is macho - it is an essential part of your masculinity. Don't let anyone make you think otherwise

4

The Step-Family

A step-family is a family in which one of the parents is not the natural father or mother of one or more of the children. There are many ways in which this situation can come about.

When two people have children, they do not always spend the rest of their lives together. One of the parents can be left looking after all the children perhaps because of divorce, separation or even the death of their partner. For a period of time they may be the only adult bringing up the children (as a one parent family). Eventually though, they may meet someone else who agrees to share the household responsibilities as a new partner or new spouse. And so the step-family is born.

Q: Is a step-family a good thing? Or, to put it another way, is it as good as the traditional family unit?

In a word - yes! Any sort of family unit that works is a good thing. It is no better or worse than any other living arrangement.

We are all social animals and as we move through life we encounter a host of different people - some through long term, lasting relationships and others just for a short period of time. Whether we love, hate, like or despise these people, they all have something in common - the experiences of meeting them all help enrich our own lives. Similarly, in a step-family, a new mother figure or a new father figure can bring much to the others in the family - provided, of course, it is through love, patience and support.

But don't think a step-family is going to be an overnight success. Like any partnership, it has to be worked at - ground rules have to be established, territory has to be redefined and relationships have to be developed. It all takes time as everyone learns about each other.

The key to eventual success is to involve the children all along the way through discussion in anything that is going to affect them. And your arrival as a step-parent will certainly do that. So, be open with them; share your feelings and worries with each other.

The Special Problems of being a Step-Parent

Making Room: The arrival of a step-parent into the household will create a need for a shift of territory. Everyone will have to make room for the new adult parent and possibly for any children they bring with them as well. This could mean anything from sharing wardrobes, cupboard space, bedrooms and beds to getting used to extra nick-knacks on the hand basin and on top of the dressing table. More importantly, it also means making room for a new set of likes and dislikes, feelings and needs.

Fitting In: It will take you time as a step-parent to learn everything you need to know in order to fit in with the new family. You will have to find out what are the rules of the house and it will be the unwritten ones that are likely to give you the most problem. Who uses the bathroom first in the morning; who sits where at the table or in the living room; who decides what to watch on television are some of the questions you may only find the answers to the hard way.

Find out how far you are expected to go with regard to discipline and the laying down of rules. Make sure the children know where both you and they stand.

Of course, you will bring your own sets of rules and values to the family and they too will have to discover what they are and learn to respect them. You may have personal belongings you don't want others to touch or look at; you may have strong views on smoking in the house; you may have times when you want to be left alone.

Being Accepted: 'Fools rush in where angels fear to tread' is an apt proverb here. The new step-parent may be tempted to rush headlong into taking over the running of the family and everyone's lives in it from the first day. To do this will be as fraught with danger as running blindfolded through a minefield.

You have to tread carefully and spend many years earning your place as a respected adult member of the family. Along the way, you may encounter a mixture of feelings from your step-children as they adjust to you being around. They may be jealous of the time you spend with their natural parent believing that they are deliberately being ignored. This could result in a bout of attention seeking - yours or your partner's.

On the other hand, you may not be very keen to muck in with bringing up baby or your partner might resent the attention you are heaping on the children. They may feel you are trying to take over because you feel you can do it better. If you have replaced an ex-partner or a divorced parent you will have to make it clear that you haven't usurped their previous position. Rather, you are an extra parent who is there to help.

Unfortunately, you could find that the ex-parent strongly resents your being around and may try to turn the children against you. There is no easy answer to this other than to keep calm and let time take its course. Continue to emphasise to both the children and the 'other' parent that you'd prefer to co-operate for everyone's sake and especially for the children's benefit.

The children themselves will have to come to terms with your presence when it comes to dealing with outsiders such as their friends and teachers. With patience, you will be accepted. So, the rule of thumb is to be open with the family and allow yourself to gradually become involved in a way that doesn't come across as being threatening.

Q: What have you to offer the family in your position as a step-parent?

If the previous section sounded negative and alarming, don't worry - you have *lots* to offer - given time! A few ideas of what you can do are listed below (in no particular order):

✪ Help with the household chores
✪ Take a turn at reading or telling bed time stories
✪ Provide a personal chauffeur service to shuttle the children to and from Brownies, Scouts, the school disco, the cinema...

✪　Be ready to play games with the children. You will learn most about each other when you share activities

✪　Be another friend for the children to talk with and to share secrets with. Remember, if there's a problem the best thing is to talk about it

✪　Share your own special talents with the family - you may be a dab hand at cooking lasagne and chips; a whizkid at football or tennis; a brilliant artist, musician, car mechanic, DIY expert or horse rider

✪　Show that you are someone it is safe to be with

✪　Take an interest in what the children are doing

One Parent Families - and do they work?

A one parent family is simply one in which the children are living with only one of their parents. The other parent may have died, divorced or disappeared or there may have been a conscious decision to be an unmarried parent.

And yes, they do work. But, as with step-families there are special problems a lone parent will have to cope with.

The problems of being a single parent
and how to deal with them

Breadwinner or Parent? As a lone parent you will have to cope with all the jobs normally covered by two partners. These include earning enough income to live on (whether from state benefits or from wages), be around for the children when they need you and coping with all the domestic tasks of running a household and family.

Loneliness and tiredness are likely to be two states you suffer from frequently.

You can feel terribly alone being the only adult in the house trying to juggle all the needs of the family. Who do you turn to when you're not well, feeling depressed or just feel you can't cope? There is no easy answer but there are people and organisations that can help (see Help List for a selection of national contacts).

One Parent: Being the only parent is a potential problem in itself as you will have to be both mother and father to your children. However, this can be an advantage in one respect in that the children are less likely to be caught up in the flak of two parents arguing furiously with each other.

In your 'mother' role you may have to spend more time on domestic tasks - cleaning, washing, shopping and looking after young children. You may need to give more time for cuddling them, for talking to them, for dealing with cuts, grazes and headaches as well as being there to listen to their chatter.   In your 'father' role, you will have sole responsibility for all the family's money matters, dealing with repairs, maintaining the car and so on.

Loneliness: When there are two parents, you have someone to share your worries, decisions and feelings with. As a single parent, you may have no other adult in the house to talk to or on whom you can unload your worries.   Combat this enforced isolation by looking outside your immediate home for the support you might have come to expect from a resident adult partner. There may be grandparents, brothers, sisters or cousins nearby who you can see regularly. One or more of your immediate neighbours may be a good alternative, especially if they have children of their own. Meet other single parents in your locality and find out if there are local One Parent support groups or clubs you can join.

What you mustn't do is shut yourself away with your children, don a martyr's sackcloth and ashes and tell the world you don't need help from anyone. Because it won't be true.

The Ex-Partner: If you are a single parent because of divorce or separation, you may still have to have regular contact with your ex-partner/spouse. You may have custody of the children but the other parent is likely to have regular visiting rights or access as well. This is not going to be easy especially if you resist the arrangement. It is important for your children to know that, just because you no longer share your life and love with their other parent, it is still possible for them to love and be loved by both parents.

There are positive aspects to regular visits by the children's other parent and it's up to you to make use of them.

✿ Use the visits as an opportunity to discuss and share problems that affect the children

✿ The other parent may be only too willing to buy them items of clothing they need that you can't afford or to take them to places you haven't time for

✿ Use these times as a chance for you to have a breather. When you are the only parent, these times can be precious. Ideally you should try to spend this time doing something you want to do though, of course, you could totally exhaust yourself by cleaning the house from top to bottom while everyone is out

Gay and Lesbian Families

The idea of children being brought up by homosexual or mixed race parents is one that is surrounded by controversy. But the howls of protest that can greet this suggestion are unlikely to be rooted in any sensible arguments but rather in the protestors' own deeply felt prejudices.

But can they work?

Of course they can! Any family that is built on love, trust and respect will work.

A gay or lesbian couple who truly love each other make just as good parents as their heterosexual equivalents (see the film *The Birdcage* starring Robin Williams if you don't believe me). Problems along the way will be largely similar to those encountered by any parents, by single parents and by step-parents. In addition, they will have to combat possible prejudices from other families, adults or children in the neighbourhood.

Mixed Race Families

The 1991 Census shows that 5.5% of the population is made up of people from the ethnic minorities and that one pre-school child in five is now of a mixed race.

Mixed race parents may need to compromise over cultural or religious differences. Again, the key to overcoming the problems is to talk about them and, more importantly not to use the children as pawns. In the end, they will choose which religion they want to be part of and which aspects of each parent's cultural background they want to adopt. For the time being, share your different cultures with everyone rather than force them to accept them. Children are remarkably receptive and they nearly always respond to new or different ways of doing things.

5

Coping With Conflict

One of the most valuable ways in which you can improve the quality of life in your family is to tackle the way you deal with conflict. Arguments and quarrels are all part and parcel of any active relationship, so there's nothing wrong with a healthy disagreement.

Unless, that is, it ends in a black eye, broken dishes, a week long sulk or the imposition of punishments. When these or worse are regular occurrences, something needs to be done.

Fierce arguments that get out of hand can unleash anger like an uncontrollable forest fire destroying everyone and everything in its path. While anger is a natural human emotion, it must be restrained.

Whether the argument is between parents, between parent and child or between the children themselves, the ways it can be contained are pretty much the same.

Keeping the Peace - strategies aimed at preventing the outbreak of war in the family home

When there is a sudden outburst of anger the first priority is to defuse and contain the situation. This requires a cooling off period, for nothing constructive can be achieved until the rage has passed. Of course, if you're the one who's angry it's easier said than done so everyone in the family must be aware of strategies they can use to defuse the situation. Some ideas are given below but this list is by no means exhaustive. Whatever works for you should be added to it.

Dealing with anger between you and your partner

✿ When confronted with your partner's anger, walk away from the outburst saying you will talk about the problem when they've had a chance to calm down. This cooling off period should be regarded as a temporary measure to enable you both to shake off the worst of the rage, not as a way of running away from or going into a sulk about the problem

✿ Apologise. If you can see you are at least partly at fault, there is no harm in saying you're sorry. Nevertheless, you should be careful not to compromise yourself too often this way in case you start to do it every time there's an angry outburst. There may be instances when you're not to blame and your partner is merely exploiting your readiness to back down

✿ At the earliest possible moment (that is, when you are both ready), sit down near to your partner and talk out the reasons for the anger

✿ Be positive. Clarify the situation by looking at both points of view. Your aim is to solve the problem not to cast blame or to heap on the guilt

✿ Stick to the point and don't get diverted away from the main issue by bringing up past grievances

✿ Above all, listen to what your partner has to say but make sure you're given the opportunity to give your side. At this stage avoid throwing accusations back and forth between you

✿ Keep at it until you've got to the bottom of the problem and how to deal with it. In the majority of cases you will both have to be prepared to compromise

✿ Call a truce while you work things out, especially if you still need to talk more about the problem. End the discussion with a hug and a kiss even if you haven't finished getting to the bottom of the problem

✿ When the same problem keeps rearing its angry head, it may be an idea to write down both your feelings and thoughts as well as the reasons that lead up to the outburst. Then work back and see how each of you can avoid making the same mistakes

An example situation - you repeatedly get angry over the time your partner comes home from the pub. You both end up going to bed in a rage because you always have a row about it.

By sitting down during the day (say over mid morning coffee), you can both write down why each of you get angry.

You might say it's because:
✿ he comes home drunk every time
✿ he comes home late

✿ it happens six days a week
✿ you always have to stay home and baby sit

He might say:

✿ he's always gone to the pub in the evening
✿ all his friends are at the pub
✿ he likes two or three pints every night after a hard day at work
✿ what's the harm in it. He's always in before half eleven and he doesn't smoke or gamble
✿ he's fed up with your nagging him about it every night when he comes home

Hopefully, by the time you've both written down your thoughts you'll begin to see the other side of the coin. You will see that he's only doing what he's always done, that it's his normal way of unwinding, that he doesn't drink to excess and that yes, you do have a tendency to nag him about it.

He, on the other hand, should see that he's being unreasonable expecting to carry on socialising as if he was still a single man and perhaps he could try to spend more evenings involving you.

This will lead to further compromises if all continues to go well. He will limit his visits to the pub to three or four nights a week, he will stay home with you on the other evenings or, better still, arrange a baby sitter so that you can join him. You, on the other hand will avoid standing at the front door with the rolling pin but will try to be more welcoming when he does come home. Perhaps you can encourage him to invite his friends to the house or he may stay home one evening to allow you to go out in the evening with your friends.

At the heart of the problem will be your feeling left out and lonely. You may also be worried about how much money is being spent on drink and you may be worried that he's turning into an alcoholic. He on the other hand may be concerned that he has to maintain his macho image if he's not going to be turned into a hen-pecked husband the moment he gives in. By talking the problem out you may begin to understand what each of you is thinking.

Dealing with angry children

Children's outbursts tend to be more frequent but shorter and quickly forgotten about. In most cases the following may be all you have to do to defuse the situation.

✿ Separate the angry parties and send them into opposite corners of the room or into separate rooms to cool off

✿ Then, sit the children down and give each the chance to explain why they are angry

✿ If you think one of them has acted unfairly then say so and explain why. Ask this child to apologise and then get them both to make up

✿ Change the activity and do something different. Perhaps you can briefly start them off and even spend a little time playing with them

✿ If the argument is more serious then you may need to act as a mediator using similar techniques to those described on the previous page. Let them go through the same process you would use in a dispute with your partner and try and talk them through the problem

Discipline

You may think from reading the above, that there is never going to be a need for disciplinary action because all you have to do is 'talk through the situation'. To a large extent that will be true but there are still going to be times when you will need to discipline your children.

Discipline is the systematic training and, when necessary, punishment you will use to ensure that your children obey your rules and accept your authority. Too much discipline will make you authoritarian and over strict; too little will spoil the children.

The ultimate aim of discipline is to help your children become independent citizens who will abide by society's rules, act responsibly and fairly and who will take control of their own actions. What it is not for is the establishment of your dictatorial authority simply because you are bigger and stronger than them.

Legally, parents are still allowed to use corporal punishment even though it is now banned in schools. However, if you overdo it by beating your child black and blue, the chances are that an assault charge will be made against you and your children taken into care. What is reasonable corporal punishment will depend upon many factors - the age of the child, the severity of the misdemeanour, the method you use to punish and the frequency by which you employ it. A quick smack on the leg of a four year old child who has poked a knife into the electricity socket or who has stolen sweets from the supermarket may be quite acceptable. To beat a fifteen year old with a stick for coming home late is not.

Here are some do's and don't's regarding discipline:
✿ Establish a set of rules that are fair and reasonable. Make it clear that you expect your children to obey and respect the rules. Be open to discussion as your children grow up so that rules can be changed by mutual agreement
✿ Be consistent. Make it clear what is and is not acceptable behaviour
✿ When a rule is broken by accident you should not punish
✿ When punishment is necessary, do it straight away. The threat of punishment later or 'when your father gets home' should be avoided

✪ If you are very angry do not use any sort of physical punishment. The chances are you will be too rough or will smack too hard

✪ Use corporal punishment sparingly. Always use a different method if at all possible. However, if you say 'I will smack you if you do that again' and she/he does, you have to do it. If you don't, your child will know that your rules and commands can be bent

✪ Never hit a child around the head

✪ Make up as soon as possible after any sort of punishment has been administered. It is important that your children know you still love them even though something they did had made you cross. A hug, kiss or a kindly word will show you have forgiven and that they are no longer excluded from you

✪ The most important thing you can do to discipline your children is set a good example yourself. Your behaviour and your methods of punishment are likely to be copied

✪ Always apologise if you've got it wrong

6

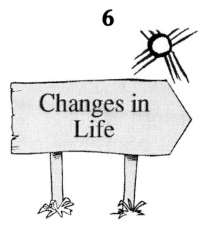

Changes in Life

Chapter 2 outlined the changes brought about by your children's growth and development and their effect on the family. In chapter 7 you can read about how to cope with a variety of disasters ranging from death and illness to debt and eviction. This chapter concentrates on major events that are likely to be planned for and yet will still have a great effect on the family.

The birth of another child

This major event, especially if it is the birth of your second child, will greatly affect the rest of the family but the first born in particular. Up until now, your first born child will have been kingpin in the household, expecting one hundred percent of your time and affection. Now, suddenly there is a baby in the house demanding everyone's attention.

As parents it will be vital for you to continue to be aware of your first-born's needs and to actively involve him/her in the process of welcoming a new member into the family. He/she will be greatly interested in everything that's gone on and will want to help wherever possible. Eventually, the new baby will become a companion for your first-born so it is worth fostering positive feelings from the start. The baby should not be seen as a threat to the first-born's position nor as a rival for your affection.

Nevertheless, there are bound to be times when demand for your attention clashes and the new baby's needs take priority. For example, it is common for mothers to find their first-born being particularly naughty when they are feeding the baby. You may also find an increase in tearfulness, disturbed sleep patterns and loss of appetite.

When there are two parents in the home, this event can provide a golden opportunity for the father to develop a closer relationship with the first-born child. While mother is busy feeding the baby, father can make a point of spending time with the older child - playing games, talking, going for a walk, doing household jobs together.

In the end, children with brothers and sisters are more likely to grow up with the ability to share, co-operate and make friendships. While they are learning to get on with each other, it is just as important for you to praise them for getting on well together as to scold them for arguing or fighting. Equally important will be your ability to treat all the children fairly. To favour one child in particular can develop deep seated resentments inside the other children in the family.

Granny comes to stay

There may come a time when an elderly relative of the family comes to live in your house. This may be due to the death of their partner or because they now need to live with people who can care for them.

Don't assume this can happen without proper consultations with the rest of the family. You may be delighted to think of your mother coming to live with you. Your partner, however, could be less than enamoured with the idea. You should only agree to this happening if everyone is in agreement and if it really is a practical solution. It may be that the only way she can come to stay is if one of your children gives up their bedroom. Make sure you find out what your children really think about the suggestion. They may say it's okay but deep down resent having their personal space reduced.

Once granny has moved in, there will need to be some adjustments from everyone. Granny herself must be made aware of the ground rules that ensure the smooth running of the household. Unless she is infirm, she should be expected to adhere to these rules and to take her share of helping around the house. By contrast, granny will have major adjustments to make herself. She will have given up her own home and her right to organise it exactly how she wanted to come and live with you. She may not be too happy at having to abide by your rules.

There will be no easy answer, particularly if granny is also a cantankerous old bat, but the only real way is through discussion. You must all feel able to bring out in the open any difficulties or problems. If, for example, you dislike granny's habit of smoking in the living room, then she must know it isn't acceptable. Then go on to work out how she can continue smoking without upsetting the rest of the family. Perhaps she can be allowed to smoke in one room of the house or at particular times of the day.

Moving house

From time to time, you may decide to move to a different house. This may be because you need to live in another area due to your starting a new job or simply because your present house is too small.

The older your children are, the harder it will be for them to accept a move. By the time they are seven years old and upwards, your children will have begun to build up a circle of friends and relationships outside the home. They may also be settled in their school and enjoying everything it has to offer them. Children under five, on the other hand will be more able to take a move in their stride.

As with any important planned change to your family circumstances, always involve your children in the discussions and preparations for the move. If this means changing schools, make sure you do all you can to accommodate your children's opinions. For example, if you're not moving too far, it may be possible for your children to continue attending the same school, at least until the end of the current school year. New children in a class are always at a disadvantage if they begin half way through the year when all the others in the class know the ropes. But starting in a new school at the beginning of a school year does help reduce some of the uncertainty as all the children in the class will also be learning to find their way with a new teacher and a new timetable.

When you do have to make a complete break of area, encourage your children to continue with one or two of their friendships. This can be achieved by inviting them to stay once you have settled in, regular telephone calls and letter writing. An option to consider if one of your children is over sixteen is the possibility of him/her lodging with friends in the old area. This may be essential if a crucial stage in education has been reached.

When you're inspecting prospective properties, either to rent or to buy, make sure again that everyone in the family is involved. Listen to what they have to say and if they hate a house you like, find out why. They may have seen something you've overlooked. Unless you have no choice in the matter, always try to plump for a house everybody is enthusiastic about.

Starting a new school

You don't necessarily have to move areas for this to happen. It may simply be the normal transition from primary to secondary school. In which case, both schools should have a number of schemes in place to help both the children and the parents adjust to the move. Make sure you make the time to attend any special induction days or evenings as it will be there that you will familiarise yourself with what the new school has to offer and what it expects from you.

If, on the other hand, you decide to transfer your children to a different school for other reasons, it will be up to you to ensure you receive all the information you need to make a smooth transition. It will certainly be a good idea for you all to visit the intended school beforehand to get a feel of the place. (See section on 'educational matters' in chapter 11 for more information on what to look for in a school.) Be sure to monitor the settling in process, especially in the first few months, to make certain that there are no major problems.

Starting a new job

When you begin working for a new employer, there are many adjustments to be made and you are likely to be more tired in the initial months. Because of this, the rest of the family may have to make allowances for you.

A new job can mean many things - a different monthly wage packet, different working hours, more work being brought home, or the commandeering of the family car for business purposes. With regular family discussions any problems these changes might create should be manageable with time.

When it's one of your children starting a new job, or even their first job, you too will have to make adjustments. You will no longer be able to assume that they can automatically babysit for you when you want an evening out or that they can continue helping with household chores to the same degree as before. More than ever you will have to treat them as adults and as equals.

But this does have its consequences on the now working child. He/she is now earning a regular income in their own right. If they continue to live at home, you must insist that a reasonable proportion of their earnings is put into the family purse - even if you don't actually need it. One of the responsibilities of being an adult is that you have to pay your fair share towards your living expenses - rent, heating, food, council tax and so on. If you don't insist on a regular contribution for their keep, your child will quickly develop a distorted view of money, ie that it is only there for their own personal pleasures (even when you don't need this contribution, you can always invest it in a savings account of some sort and then produce it when it's needed for the down payment for a flat or a car).

Divorce and Separation

All a divorce does is end the marriage contract. It doesn't sort out the problems surrounding the divorce.

It is generally agreed that the biggest victims of any divorce or separation are the children. If you have reached the stage when it is too late to avoid splitting up from your spouse or partner, you do need to seriously consider what is going to be best for the children.

Recent research is largely in agreement on the following points:

- ✿ Children of divorced or separated parents are more likely to experience drugs or teenage pregnancy
- ✿ Most children hope their separated parents will get back together again (even if you and they know this is impossible)
- ✿ Quality of family life with one or both parents is more important than the parents staying together 'for the sake of the children'
- ✿ The most important thing both parents can do is spend time with their children

Whatever the reasons for the split, it is advisable to seek counselling help and advice to make sure this really is the best thing to do (some contacts are given in the Help List). Using a family mediation service at any time to discuss and clarify the issues can prevent disputes getting out of hand and can help keep the legal costs to a minimum.

Remember that children are people not possessions. Try to bring them into discussions and listen to what they have to say. Be prepared to let older children decide with whom they choose to live but also accept they may change their mind later on. And whoever they end up living with, make sure they are not either physically or emotionally prevented from seeing their other parent as often as they want.

When violence or abuse is the reason for the split none of the above may apply. In this instance your first priority is to ensure safety and protection for you and the children (see Help List for emergency helpline contacts).

7

When Disaster Strikes - Coping with Crises

However much you plan, however much you scrimp and save, however careful you are, it is unlikely that you and your family will pass through life without meeting a variety of disasters head on.

Disasters can take many forms and the following list just gives a few of the more common ones.

Look at this list and mentally tick off all those events that have a) happened to you personally, b) have happened to someone else in your family and c) that have occurred in the past five years.

- ☼ Death of a parent, child or grandparent
- ☼ The onset of a serious illness or disability
- ☼ Involvement in a major accident
- ☼ The break up of a relationship and the family home
- ☼ Redundancy and unemployment
- ☼ Serious debt
- ☼ Loss of the family home due to fire, flood or repossession
- ☼ Burglary
- ☼ A member of your family is convicted of a criminal offence

The point of this exercise is to show that nothing is

ever quite so bad as it appears at the time once time has been allowed to heal. We don't forget these major events but we do find a place for them that lets us get on with our present lives.

Some of the more common crisis events are examined below.

Death and Bereavement

This is probably the most difficult crisis to cope with and there is never going to be one single way that is right for everyone. When a close member of your family dies, you don't know how you are going to react. You may be utterly grief-stricken for weeks or months. On the other hand, you may find you don't react at all and that your grief only comes out much later. It is important to realise that there is no right or wrong way of dealing with bereavement and don't let others cajole you into behaving differently to the way you actually want to. They aren't you and they cannot know what you are feeling.

Whilst most death occurs in old age, a significant number of people die young and suddenly from a variety of causes. Death always comes as a shock, even when it occurs at the end of a long and painful illness. Apart from shock, you are also likely to experience panic, disbelief and a sense of numbness and loss. You may not be able to talk about it to anyone let alone provide comfort to others in your family. It's doubly difficult giving comfort when you actually need the very same support yourself.

It is important for none of you to bottle up your feelings indefinitely. If necessary, each of you must find someone who can help and this will possibly mean going outside the immediate family to a friend, a distant relative, a teacher, a work colleague, a priest or a bereavement counsellor.

Helping your family cope with death

✪ Be truthful. Listen to your children's questions and try to give direct answers. Although you may feel some questions are too direct or inappropriate you should nevertheless try to give a straight answer. After all, you are aiming to guide the asker in their own journey through grief. They must know, for example, that the deceased will never return

✪ Provide reassurance. Give as much support, sympathy and comfort as you can. Hug and hold each other; cry together

✪ Mourn your loss together. Involve everyone, however young, in this process of mourning. Anyone left out may find it more difficult to accept that a death has occurred. If you can't all go to the funeral together, make a point of visiting the graveside or crematorium soon after

✪ Celebrate the life of the deceased. Share your memories and try to keep them positive. Look through old photographs and remember your experiences together

✪ Let your children express their feelings in their own way. This might include playing out with friends as if everything was normal. Never make them feel guilty if they don't show their grief in the same way as you

Death of a pet
For many children the death of a family pet will be their first experience of death so it will be important to treat it as seriously as the death of a human being. It can certainly be as devastating as the death of a brother, sister or parent. The pain and grief caused by the loss will be just as real and just as difficult to bear.

The onset of a serious illness or disability (perhaps as the result of an accident)

This event may require everyone to rethink the whole future of the family. Everyone must avoid casting blame or guilt but rather accept the new situation as a challenge for the family to overcome together. There will undoubtedly have to be considerable sacrifices made by all members of the family many of which are likely to be unwelcome.

✿　If the illness or disability is long term or permanent, one of the adults may have to give up their paid employment to become a full time carer

✿　The family may have to consider moving house, say from a house with lots of stairs to a bungalow

✿　The children may have to take on extra routine tasks and chores

✿　The family income is likely to be considerably reduced - disability or sickness benefits rarely compensate for the loss of an earned income

Redundancy and Unemployment

This will have two main consequences - a loss of income and a loss of face for the parent who has lost their job.

For many people, being made redundant is likened to a bereavement. Initially you don't know whether to be angry, depressed, frustrated or resentful. Hopefully, these will be fleeting feelings and you will be able to put them and any nostalgia you may have for the lost job behind you. Take a fresh look at everything you have to offer and make the decision to make a fresh start.

You won't know how long the situation is going to last so don't waste time doing nothing because you believe something will turn up tomorrow. It rarely does! The only way another job is likely to turn up is if you get out there and start looking for it.

✪ Financially, you should immediately investigate your family's entitlement to benefits, which cannot usually be backdated. Even if you think you might not be entitled to any state benefits, it is always worth visiting the Job Centre to 'sign on' or contacting your local Citizens Advice Bureau for advice

✪ Loss of face is a more difficult aspect to deal with. For someone who has spent years developing a career, to suddenly have nothing to do will come as a shock. Many people in this situation wallow in self-pity and spend most of the day semi-comatose in front of the television. They are not prepared to consider any job unless it carries the same salary as before and is roughly in the same field of work. Everyone in the family is advised to stay away and to not talk about the problem. This state of affairs, if it is allowed to continue for long, is a surefire recipe for disaster

When job loss occurs to you, think through why it happened - perhaps you're no longer suited to the work; perhaps there is less need for this type of work. And perhaps it's a heaven sent opportunity to radically change your life. If you hadn't lost your job what would you be doing? Probably continuing at the same desk, the same production line, in front of the same blackboard, at the wheel of the same vehicle until you come to retire. So, yes, it is important to get back to work and find another job as soon as possible but it could also provide the chance for you to do something completely different - you could retrain, develop new skills and interests and even try something completely new.

Work isn't only about earning enough to pay the mortgage, though this is still important. Work is also about giving and sharing your talents (many of which you probably don't even know you have); it's a way of being part of the wider community and of making a positive contribution to society.

While you're unemployed, consider the merits of voluntary work. There is a host of charities and organisations crying out for people like you to work for them. You may need to tell the Job Centre what you are doing and you may have to stop the voluntary work at a moment's notice if the right sort of job comes along. Becoming involved in voluntary work can be rather like the wild card in the pack because it can frequently lead you along a different route into a new career.

Serious Debt

This can creep up on you and take you unawares. You may have thought you were coping and then the County Court Summons plops on to the doormat. The question is, is it too late to do anything about it?

In 99 out of a 100 cases of debt problems the answer is no. It is rarely too late to bale yourself out provided you follow a few simple guidelines:

- ✿ Act early - as soon as there is a problem, talk to the people you owe money to
- ✿ Draw up a budget sheet of your income and expenditure. From this you should be able to see what you can realistically afford to pay
- ✿ Offer what you can afford and pay it even while negotiations are going on
- ✿ Taking out another loan to pay off your debts is generally not to be recommended - you just end up paying interest on interest
- ✿ Visit the Citizens Advice Bureau to obtain free help, advice and support. They can help you with all stages of your negotiations

✿ Don't ignore a County Court Summons - get help from the CAB

Remember: The longer you leave any debt problem the worse it is likely to get.

Losing Your Home

Whether you lose your home because of fire, flood or repossession you will have one over-riding priority - to get your family rehoused as quickly as possible. If your house is properly insured, you should find the insurance company will have a policy to get another roof over your head as quickly as possible. Make sure you know what the policy is and memorise the name of the insurance company.

✿ To start with, you need to find somewhere temporary and find it fast. Where can you go? 1) a nearby hotel or guest house; 2) split up the family between several neighbours; 3) go and stay with a relative or friend

✿ Next you have to gauge how long you are going to need temporary accommodation for. If it's a matter of a week or so, your friend, relative or neighbour may be willing for you to stay with them. If it's longer - say two or three months, you may need to consider 1) a short term let obtained through an estate agent; 2) a mobile home park; 3) a hotel; 4) approaching your local authority for help

✿ When your house is repossessed by a mortgage lender or landlord or a short term tenancy comes to an end, you will be looking for something more permanent. Usually, you will have a minimum of at least one month's notice of your leaving or eviction date. Don't wait until the day before but get on to it straight away

✿ Your notice to quit can be presented to the local authority or housing association as soon as you receive it. Provided you have children in the family, there is a statutory right to be rehoused by the local authority (unless, of course they are the ones who are evicting you). There are many rules and regulations that also apply but you shouldn't be put off. Go and apply anyway but still keep looking yourself

Losing your house can be like a bereavement. But once you have lost it, there is nothing to be gained in wallowing in self pity. The best you can do for yourself and family is to get on and do something. And if you're not sure what to do next, go to your nearest CAB for advice.

Burglary and Theft

No-one wants their house burgled and no-one thinks it will happen to them. The best advice is to go for prevention by making your home secure - good locks on doors and windows, security coding valuables, installing an alarm system. The police provide good advice and will often visit your home to discuss what you can do. Also, make sure you are properly insured.

However, even the best security is no guarantee if a thief is determined to break in. What can you do then?

✿ Resist the temptation to 'have a go' if you discover a thief still in your house. Your lives are far more important than your possessions. For the majority of burglars it will be enough to make a lot of noise to show them you are there. This should frighten them away

✿ Call the police immediately but wait until they arrive before you start trying to clear up. The less you touch the more chance there is that the police will find any incriminating evidence left behind

✿ As soon as you are able, make an inventory of everything that has been taken or damaged. Then notify your insurance company

- ☼ If credit cards, cheque books or other documents have been taken, notify the appropriate bank or organisation
- ☼ Make your house secure as quickly as possible, especially at the point of entry. Thieves have been known to return
- ☼ Put everything into perspective. Once the shock has worn off, remember that your family's health and well being are a million times more important than any amount of stolen TVs, videos and jewellery
- ☼ If, however, you continue to feel frightened, confused, insecure or even ashamed, contact the Victims' Helpline on **0171 729 1252** for advice and support.

Crime in the family

Every criminal has a family - parents, spouse or children. You can't turn back the clock - the crime has been committed and sentence passed. But for the present and immediate future, you have to learn to live with having a member of your family who is a convicted criminal.

- ☼ One of the most important things you can do is to provide support for whoever is the criminal. You may not be able to forget what has happened but you certainly should try to forgive. A positive attitude to the situation and to the future, without condoning the crime, is more likely to help prevent the same thing ever happening again. If you reject that person completely, there will be a much higher chance that he/she will go out and commit more crimes
- ☼ Depending upon the crime, you may initially have problems with neighbours and work colleagues who blame you for the crime. Similarly, you may actually blame yourself. Whatever your feelings on the subject, get help from Victims' Support, the Prisoners Families Advice & Information Network or similar organisations

8

Getting On With Each Other

Making your family work is all about getting on with each other. Apart from husband and wife or adult partners, no-one else in the family has any real choice when it comes to choosing their grandparents, brothers, sisters and even their own children.

To put it bluntly, you're stuck with them whether you like it or not. Hopefully, for most of the time you're going to be happy living with the other members of your family.

Because you can't choose your nearest and dearest, you're going to have to work out ways of getting on with each other. And one way to do this is to think positive. Don't keep harping on about various irritable habits that annoy you for after all, you've probably got plenty of your own that annoy everybody else. Instead concentrate on developing sound relationships - some key pointers are listed below under the STABIL method.

The STABIL method - or how to maintain a stable relationship

Stability between partners and other members of the

family is achieved through Sharing, Talking, Accepting, Being nice, respecting everyone's Individuality and need to be on their Lonesome.

✪ **S**haring. Make an effort to put aside regular amounts of time to share with your partner and with the others in your family - go out together for a walk or to see a film; play games; sit down together to watch the same television programmes, listen to music, read or chat

✪ **T**alking. The way to deal with what appears to be a problem is not to just lay the law down but rather to talk about it. Regular discussions with your partner or with your children are another key factor in making a relationship work. Talking oils the machinery of the smooth running of the family on a day to day basis. So make sure you put aside regular amounts of time to talk - over the dinner table, while you're doing the washing up, when you're out walking the dog or a few minutes at bed time

✪ **A**ccepting each other's faults. We all have our own individual set of shortcomings and coupled with our good points, they are what make us all different. Good relationships are founded on the ability to get on with people rather than setting out to turn each other into the sort of idealistic clones found in 'The Stepford Wives'.

This is not to say that there isn't room for improvement. But it is important to distinguish between shortcomings that can be and should be tackled and those that are simply differences of opinion, attitude or preference.

For example, take the situation in which your teenage daughter likes to read Mills & Boon novellas every day. Should you try and get her to stop reading them? If the only reason for disliking this habit is because you disapprove of them, the answer has to be no. On the other hand, if you find that she is reading five or six books a day and neglects her homework as a result, it may be necessary to discuss what has increasingly come to be an obsession. Talk to her and find out why she feels she needs to read so many. It may be that she is the only girl in her class not to have had a boyfriend, she may feel out of depth with her school work, she may feel desperately lonely or it may simply be a little escapism. The solution isn't going to be stopping her from reading Mills & Boon books altogether but rather to allocate a time and a place for indulging in these harmless fantasies

☼ **Being nice.** Having a deliberate policy to be nice is a way of showing you care. It's all too easy to fall into the trap of concentrating on the faults and problems so much that all you do is criticise. So, think of ways you can do the opposite: we all thrive on a bit of flattery and praise and we all appreciate being made to feel special. You never know, some of this might rub off on the rest of the family and they could end up being nicer to each other and to you

☼ **Individuality.** Don't expect to be included in absolutely everything. Give everyone space to develop their own hobbies and interests without them feeling they have to involve everyone else in them. Respect each person's individuality and everything that goes to make it

☼ **Leaving to be alone.** Respect everybody's need for time by themselves. It's important to work out when this is and leave them to it. For example, the majority of people coming home from a hard day at work or at school will want half an hour or more to recover before being bombarded by a whole lot of questions, wants and trivial problems to sort out

Sharing, talking, giving each other space, respecting everybody's individuality, tolerating their shortcomings and being nice. These are just a few ideas for making relationships work. But do these pointers work for all relationships - between parent and child, brother and sister, grandparent and grandchild? In one word the answer is yes! Provided at least one person sets out to use these guidelines, the vast majority of relationships will work. They will work even when tackling the most cantankerous of elderly grandparents or rebellious of teenage children. In these instances, success is not going to come over night but rather you're going to develop an environment in which you can at least tolerate each other.

Parents - and how to deal with them

Your parents are going to be with you for most of your life and, if you're lucky they'll still be around when it's your turn to retire. You can look at them in two ways:

✿   As people to keep as far a way from as soon as you can
✿   As people who will always be with you and a part of you for the whole of your life

You can move to Papua New Guinea and not leave a forwarding address but all you will escape is their physical presence. Spiritually and mentally, however, they will always be with you. There is no escape from the influence they have on your subconscious and how you approach all aspects of life. And, of course, some physical aspects will be with you - the inherited shock of curly hair, brown eyes and stature, your speech, your mannerisms and so on.

Even if you opt for the first strategy, they will always be with you in some form or other. So, don't fight them but learn to live with them and hopefully learn to enjoy everything they have to offer.

As a child, getting on with your parents is unlikely to be a matter of concern for you. They are there and so are you, warts and all. QED. You just get on with it. At the same time, you will probably use the guidelines above as a matter of course. It will come naturally for you to talk to them, to share your toys with them when you ask them to play with you. (Anyway, what father needs an excuse to play with your cars and your train set?)

As you get older, you'll be increasingly left to your own devices - to watch children's TV, to play with your toys on your own or because your parents are too busy. This natural progression allows you to develop your own individuality and need for time on your own. As a child, you should be tucked up in bed well before your parents retire to theirs. Apart from the fact that you need more sleep than they do, these extra hours in bed also naturally give your parents much needed time for themselves. Of course, all they might do with the time is sit comatose in front of the television but that's their choice.

The younger you are, the easier it is to follow the relationship rules. This is mainly because you have little choice in the running of things anyway. But what happens when you get older?

The move from childhood through adolescence into adulthood is one of the more difficult periods in your life both from your point of view and from that of those around you. For this reason the whole of the next chapter is devoted to your teenage years.

As an adult, your dealings with your parents need to be on a more equal footing as adult to adult. This can be difficult to achieve if there's been no transition from the 'I'm your father, do as I say' scenario you could routinely expect when you were nine years old.

Nevertheless, the only real way to live in close proximity with your parents now is to gently assert yourself. Make it clear where the boundaries lie but be prepared to compromise as well. You should no longer expect to be told what time you should come home in the evening, what you should wear or what you should do with your spare time. On the other hand, and especially if you continue to share the same home as your parents, it is not unreasonable to follow rules about cleanliness, tidiness and noisiness around the house.

More suggestions for a smooth running household are given in chapter 10 on grandparents.

Brothers and Sisters

You've only got to look in the Bible to see that getting on with your brother or sister can cause a lot of heartache and hardship. In Genesis, you can read how Cain murdered his brother Abel (chapter 4); how Jacob duped his brother Esau out of his birthright (chapter 27) and how Joseph was sold to the Egyptians by his brothers (chapter 37). These stories are linked by one emotion - jealousy.

Jealousy is probably at the heart of many of the disputes between brothers and sisters. When one brother sees another being favoured, he decides it's not fair which in turn can lead to feelings of jealousy. The resultant display of bad tempered sulking and tantrums however is unlikely to achieve anything positive.

One of the fundamental facts of life is that life is never fair and you shouldn't expect it to be. We are all different and we all have our own role to play.

It's much better to be pleased when your brother or sister does well. And when good fortune strikes you, share it with your brothers and sisters.

Although many parents unwittingly encourage rivalry between their children for example by comparing school reports, you should resist the temptation to compete at every level with your brothers and sisters. By applying the STABIL formula you are more likely to get on together.

Share your toys, sweets and time; accept they may be better than you at sport, work or whatever; respect their individuality and tolerate their bad points and above all be nice to them.

9

The Teenager's Point of View

Between the ages of twelve and twenty, getting on with your parents can become extremely difficult for a number of reasons. Your parents may not have realised how much you have grown up and how much you have changed. They quite probably still see you as the sweet little seven year old who does as she's told and never argues or answers back.

You, on the other hand, may not realise how much you are changing either. At some stage in your teenage years you will undergo the changes of puberty which physically metamorphose you from a child to an adult. This in turn will contribute to the turmoil of thoughts and feelings churning around inside you. During these years too, you will discover that your parents are just ordinary mortals and you're likely to see this by focusing on their shortcomings. Being nice to them becomes harder as you come into more conflict with them. Sharing is the last thing you want to do - anyhow, the chances are they don't want to share your new found interest in everything that goes to make up the youth sub-culture.

It's a sad state of affairs that more and more teenagers leave home at sixteen or seventeen simply because neither they nor their parents can tolerate each other. Leaving home at the right time of course is desirable. Traditionally, the wedding ceremony was the chief way this was achieved. Both parents said goodbye as they gave away their respective offspring. The ceremony was a ritual for letting go.

Today, the wedding ceremony has largely lost this role in releasing parents from their adult children and vice versa. Even where this still takes place in families, the chances are the children will already have flown the nest. They will have gone off to university, set up home in their own flat and even had a period of time sharing their lives with a partner they cohabit with.

As a teenager you want to leave your parents' home at the right time and for the right reasons - not because you've been driven out. The hardest thing for you will be to compromise. You want to experience everything now and you don't want anyone saying you can't have or do something.

But why should you compromise? Your friends don't (or so they say). There are lots of reasons why it is in your best interest to work at getting on with your parents. Looking at it selfishly for a moment, think of what they have to offer you - free board and lodging, a laundry service (also free), a warm, comfortable home with all mod cons, interest free loans and many other services. Are all these really worth giving up for the sake of your uncompromising need to come home at all hours, to play your music loudly all night and so on?

Well, only you can answer that but I hope you will

agree that, if for no other reason, you should be wanting to stay at home for as along as possible so that you don't have to concern yourself with domestic chores and managing the finances of your own home.

But there is a price for this apparently unlimited supply of material goods, warmth, food and furnishings.

You've got a lot to cope with during your teenage years. Apart from the changes to your body, you've also got to deal with a change in attitude as people expect you to act 'more like an adult'. By this phrase, of course, they mean responsible adult, which in turn means someone like them! You've also got to deal with the hardest few years at school when you will have the largest amount of homework and studying in your life. Naturally, this extra demand on your time coincides exactly with your increased desire to get out there and enjoy yourself.

None of this has to be a battle of wills. You don't have to fight your parents and teachers over everything you do or don't do. Of course, there are bound to be disagreements and arguments but with a bit of thought they can be kept to a minimum. So what can you do? Below are some ideas on dealing with other people as well as with the changes in yourself.

✿   **S**haring. Be prepared to sacrifice some of your time to spend with your family. Don't think you can stay out all day and most of the night seven days a week and not get into some sort of trouble. So, share out your time between your various needs - doing your homework (it's got to be done so why not get it out of the way early?); being with your family at meal times, helping with chores, talking to them and listening to them (they may well be boring old fogies but they've still got plenty of good advice to help you not make the same mistakes they did); being with your friends (ration the evenings out to two or three a week)

☼ **T**alking. This is the single most important thing you can do - talk. Not shout, scream, swear and insult but talk. If you're worried about the changes going on in your body - growth of hair in new places, sexual feelings, onset of sweating, periods or spots; contraception, AIDS or drugs - talk to someone about what's going on. If you don't feel you can talk to your parents find someone else you can talk to - relative, neighbour, teacher, doctor or youth advisory agency. Alternatively, ask your doctor for leaflets and booklets on the subject. (see Help List for contact addresses). But don't depend upon your friends to answer these questions. They may know the right answer but they may also get some of the facts wrong

☼ **A**ccepting. Some of the physical changes can cause 'growing pains' and make you clumsy, moody and even frightened. Accept them as normal changes and learn to live with your new body. Part of this acceptance will come by talking about and learning to understand what's going on. Accept too, that as you grow up you have to take more and more responsibility for your actions and what you do with your life. Be tolerant - it takes them a long time to accept that you have changed for they will still think of you as their little baby

☼ **B**eing nice. However you're feeling, you've still got to live with those around you. Don't take it out on them. It's not their fault! So, show that you are there for them too if they have something they need to discuss

☼ **I**ndividuality. Develop your own style of dress, hair style, hobbies and interests but don't do them at someone else's expense. You have a right to be respected as an individual but equally so, you have to respect everyone else's right to the same. So, keep the volume control down, don't wake everybody up at two a.m. by coming in drunk and don't criticise everyone else's way of doing things just because you want to be different

☼ **L**eaving to be alone. You have a right to privacy and to be left alone when you need time by yourself. Expect others to respect your privacy but treat them with the same consideration. If you don't want people barging into your room unannounced, going through your drawers or reading your private papers, then tell them. Talk to them and ask them not to do it any more

The Parents' Point of View

Hopefully you will have read the section giving the teenager's point of view (and vice versa). If you have, you're already half way there!

As a parent you will be so busy getting on with everything concerned with running a family - job, chores, shopping, cooking, DIY and so on - that you'll miss the biggest changes going on in front of your very eyes. The person you thought was your ten year old child will suddenly have become a fourteen year old young man or woman. He/she will have a whole new set of skills, feelings, attitudes, appearance and needs. You can't rely on the 'do as I say' technique any more but will have to be ready to use a range of negotiating skills to arrive at a compromise.

Whatever you might expect from your teenage children, the onus is on you to make things work. The six point plan below may guide you through the worst of the minefield.

✿ **S**haring. You have to learn to share your teenage children with other demands on their time and with other people. They will have new friends, even a boyfriend/girlfriend; they will want to be out exploring the world on their own; they will need to spend more time on their studies than on household chores. Still keep your set of rules but be prepared to relax them and to be more flexible in your demands

✿ **T**alking. Keep the communication channels open and you can avoid World War Three! Be there for them to talk to you about their worries and fears; share your own fears and problems with them; talk with them as potential adults (rather than shout and criticise)- especially if you feel the need to discipline

✿ *Accepting.* Neither you nor they can stop them growing up. With the onset of puberty, the teenager will eventually be transformed into an adult with all the feelings, desires and needs of an adult. For a time, they are likely to be unprepared for these changes and this will greatly affect their moods. Accept that there will be wild variations in mood and temper, there will be clumsiness and there will be embarrassment. And with this acceptance be tolerant and patient

✿ *Being nice.* As well as being patient, take extra pains to be nice to them. Make sure they know you still love them and, if they will let you, give them hugs and kisses to comfort them and to show you care

✿ *Individuality.* Like it or not, your teenage child is an individual with as much right to an opinion as yourself. Laying down the law will usually achieve nothing. Listen to what they've got to say, respect their search for an identity (even if this means coming out as a gay or lesbian person) and encourage them to become more independent. In return, you should expect a similar level of respect for your wishes. There is no foolproof formula for achieving a compromise as each teenager is unique, but if this is what you set out to do the chances are you will come to some sort of agreement that is at least liveable with

✿ *Leaving alone.* You must no longer assume that you have open access to your teenage child's life, inner feelings and physical space. Respect their growing need for privacy and resist the temptation to freely go into their room or look through their private possessions

10

Grandparents

I didn't know my grandparents, for the last of them died when I was a small boy. I have little recollection of any of them other than what I was told about them or gleaned from a few tattered and faded sepia photographs.

Today's children however are far more likely to know at least one of their grandparents (if not all of them) right into adulthood. You may be lucky and have them around the house on a regular basis providing extra support and companionship for the whole family.

There can, of course, be conflict between grandparents, parents and the children where there is disagreement on what is or is not the right way to run the household. It is generally agreed that the older you get, the more set in your ways you are likely to become. Children with strict parents may have grandparents who take a more laid back and lenient view on life or vice versa. Unless proper ground rules are laid down, you could find yourself in the middle of a semi-anarchistic guerilla war - with family customs and commands being flouted and contradicted all over the place. In the end the children will suffer the most as they become confused on what is and isn't right.

To allow such a situation to develop is one that will eventually cause you a lot of heartache in later years (probably after the grandparents have died) for you will realise that a great opportunity had been lost. Grandparents in the family is a three way relationship so each viewpoint needs to be examined in turn.

The parents' angle

The grandparents in question will be either yours or your partner's own parents but by the time they become involved in your family they will be granny and grandad.

What assumptions can you make?

✿ They will undoubtedly want to be involved in your family and especially in developing a special relationship with your children, ie their grandchildren

✿ They will undoubtedly have widely differing opinions on what are the right and wrong ways of bringing up the children

If you can accept these two statements as unavoidable facts, you're half way there already. What you have to do is readily accept these facts as part of the melting pot of rules, customs, values, likes and dislikes that go together to make the family work. So, don't fight them but find a positive use for them.

✿ Tap into your parents' willingness to help - let them babysit or childmind regularly to give you a break or to go out in the evening. Ask them to help with ferrying the children to school, to the doctors or to visit their friends

✿ Let them help financially too if they are able. Bringing up a family is an expensive business and you usually have to do it at the same time as coping with the mortgage, the HP on the car. By the time many people become grandparents, they often have money to spare. Don't be afraid or ashamed to ask if you need this sort of help. After all, they can always say no if they can't afford it themselves

✪ Lay down the ground rules on rules. For example, when they are in your house, they should largely abide by your sets of rules. But if your home is also your grandparents' home or if the children are visiting their grandparents' house, you may have to be more flexible. The important point here is to talk about what is and isn't acceptable.

Try, however, to distinguish between the trivial and the essential. Having an argument simply because the children were allowed to stay up an extra hour is letting matters get out of hand. But if you find your seven year old son is being allowed to watch 18 certificate films on grandad's video then this may be an occasion to read the riot act

Apply the STABIL method and you won't go far wrong:

✪ **S**hare your children with the grandparents - look at all they have to offer and don't be clouded by feelings of jealousy

✪ **T**alk to them about all aspects of their involvement in the family

✪ **A**ccept what they have to offer your family. They have several decades of life experiences and learning things the hard way, so at least listen to what they've got to say

✪ **B**e nice to them - they only want to do what's best for you and your family. Don't treat them as outsiders but include them in the family

✪ Respect their **I**ndividuality as well as their shortcomings

✪ Don't be afraid to **L**eave them alone with your children

The grandparent's angle

One of your grandchildren's parents is your child but is now a fully fledged adult in their own right. At least, that is what they believe even if you can see they still have a long way to go before they will be as experienced as you. What assumptions can you make?

✪ You have virtually no legal rights when it comes to how your grandchildren are brought up. In other words you cannot assume that you have any say at all in the matter

✪ Your grandchildren will welcome your involvement in their lives and will want to develop a special relationship with you

As a grandparent, you will have much to offer. You have the experience of bringing up your own family, a mind full of useful advice and information on any sort of topic you care to mention and lots of time to devote to giving special attention to your grandchildren. Unfortunately, not everybody will see it this way. For, if you're not careful, it is possible for you to be considered as 'an interfering old busy body who should stay away and mind their own business'.

Here again you can apply the STABIL method to minimalise the possibilities of open warfare breaking out:

✪ **S**hare your time, knowledge and experiences with the family - but don't force them on to them

✪ **T**alk to the family members about your ideas on how to do things - but, again, don't force-feed them with your own code of practice. After all, your theory of how and when to punish a child may be diametrically opposite to that of the parents. You may think a hard slap and off to bed early is the way to treat the naughty child, whereas the parent believes it better to discuss why something is wrong. Who is to say which method is preferable? Both will have their advantages and disadvantages. But, if you feel you know a better way of dealing with a situation, there is no harm in offering it as a take-it-or-leave-it suggestion

✪ **A**ccept your son or daughter's right to bring up their children in the way they think is best. Child rearing fashions change all the time and it is unlikely that you will *ever* agree wholeheartedly with the modern methods

✪ **Be** *nice*. Remember your hard times bringing up a family - you probably also had to juggle your children's needs and demands with holding down a job and managing the house and garden. Be unstinting in your praise on how well your son and daughter in law (or vice versa) are coping with everything and make sure they know they can always come to you for help and support when they need it

✪ *Individuality* keeps the world interesting. Respect each member of the family as individuals with their own particular foibles, interests and ways of doing things

✪ **Leave** things be. Make sure you give the family plenty of space to do things without you. Develop your own interests too so that none of you feel that you are living in each other's pockets

The grandchild's point of view: What can you assume?

✪ Your parents and grandparents are going to have different ideas on how to treat you

✪ Your grandparents want to have a part in your life

If you're lucky, your grandparents will be around throughout your schooldays, when you start your first job and at your wedding. What you get out of your relationships should not depend upon how much you can get out of them in the way of money and presents (though the chances are you will do well in this area). The answer lies more in what you put into them. Here again, the STABIL method can give you some clues:

✪ **Share** your life with your grandparents. They will want to play games with you, read you stories, take you to the cinema, give you extra pocket money and buy you special presents. You have much to offer too - you can help with their household chores, go shopping for them and most of all, regularly spend time with them just for company's sake

✿ **T**alk to them about your life. They want to know what you are doing and share their experiences with you

✿ **A**ccept what your grandparents have to offer. Be thankful and remember not to take anything they give you for granted. Accept too that they may be set in their ways and have rules that have to be obeyed. But avoid playing them off against those of your parents

✿ **Be** nice to them. Don't begrudge the time you spend with them but make the most of it

✿ **I**ndividuality. Your grandparents are individuals like you - they have feelings, they have good and bad days and they have their own ways of doing things. Don't take them for granted but learn to respect them as you would want your best friend to respect you

✿ **L**eave alone. If you're spending a lot of time with your grandparents give them space to be alone, especially if they want a bit of peace and quiet for an afternoon snooze. Just your presence in the house will be enough even when you're quietly getting on with something on your own

11

Practicalities

The smooth running of the family is not solely dependent upon you all developing the right relationships with one another. There is another side that can improve matters rather like WD40's action on a creaky door hinge. This chapter briefly highlights some of life's lubricants.

Time management

- ✿ Space out and pace out - balance the allocation of time to work, rest and play; give yourselves proper breaks whether at home or at work
- ✿ Plan your week. Construct a routine that allows all the necessary jobs to be done but at the same time be flexible
- ✿ Expect everyone to play a part right from the start. Washing up, tidying up toys, helping with the cleaning should be done by everybody. Don't let your children watch television until they have cleared up their toys
- ✿ Share out other tasks so that everyone has a special responsibility - putting out the rubbish, meal preparation, ironing, DIY, lawn mowing, filling in forms and keeping a check on the household accounts

✿   Plan your shopping trips so that you only have to go once or twice a week. Keep a shopping list going so that everyone can add things to it when they run out

Labour Saving Devices

If you're not careful you can fill your house with gizmos and gadgets that are meant to save time but in fact do nothing of the sort.

A dishwasher is seen by many to be indispensable. But is it? Does it actually save time? Someone still has to load and unload it. Manual washing up is a marvellous opportunity for a family activity which you can all share in. It also gives you a chance for a quiet chat with someone.

On the other hand, a tumble drier is recommended. During those long wet winter months, you can avoid the need to have unsightly racks of wet clothes forever being dried in front of the fire.

What other labour saving gadgets are worth investing in?

✿   A microwave - a faster and more economical way of cooking. It can usefully avoid messy pans if used to cook certain dishes such as scrambled eggs or porridge. It can be used to reheat drinks or meals and for quick defrosting

✿   A wok - for quick stir-fry meals

✿   A three tier steamer - it reduces the number of cooking rings needed, is more economical and results in better tasting food

✿   A steam iron - marvellous for avoiding burn marks and for pressing clothes that are too dry

✿   Stackable storage boxes - one of the best ways of keeping children's toys contained

Convenience meals

When you're juggling your home and family with a job, you need to organise the provision of meals so that you aren't also a slave to the cooker:

✿ Encourage everyone to have a go at cooking a main meal - teenagers can produce pizza and jacket potato, a pasta dish or something based on the opening of tins or the freezer door. Younger children can, with supervision, make the toast for breakfast, set out the table or help dish up the vegetables

✿ Always keep your cupboard and fridge stocked with basics and standbys - ready-mix custard powder mixes, dried milk, stock cubes and sauces, pasta, rice, cans of beans, eggs, sandwich fillers, etc. In the freezer, if you've room, store milk, bread and all in one meals such as lasagne

✿ Keep a couple of tins filled with small cakes, flapjacks, biscuits, banana bread, etc. Keep a well filled fruit bowl and have packs of yogurt in the fridge

✿ Prepare one or two of the week's main meals in advance so that all you have to do is heat them up. Good meals to make this way include shepherd's pie, lasagne, stews, curries. Once made, fruit pies, homemade yogurt, a trifle, or gateaux can be kept for several days in the fridge to provide the sweet without too much effort

✿ Build up a family cook-book with recipes that are quick and successful as well as items each person can do. Try to make sure the basic ingredients for most of the recipes are kept stocked up

Pocket money

Money is power and using pocket money to control your children just stresses this fact. Try not to use the threat of pocket money being stopped or a bonus being given as an enticement to toe the line. Even where it is agreed that pocket money should be used to pay for a breakage, it is better to give it all and then ask for some of it back.

The earlier your children get pocket money they can control, the better will be their chances of managing their finances properly when they are older. At some stage pocket money will be transformed into an allowance. When this happens, especially if there has also been a substantial increase, you should make it quite clear what it's for. Teenage children will respect you for giving them an allowance for all their non-essential items including entertainment, non school uniform clothing and trivialities. It may also help them learn to budget their spending.

At the same time, you should be encouraging your children to save some of their pocket money. This can eventually be used for more expensive items, saved for a rainy day or kept for holiday spending money. You might choose to pay a bonus into their account based, say, on ten percent of their savings over a six month period.

Avoid giving pocket money as a reward or enticement for doing ordinary household chores though you might be able to employ them for special one off jobs such as painting a fence, waxing the car or cutting the hedge.

If your money is tight, you may not be able to match the going rate reportedly received by your children's peers. In this situation, explain your difficulties and if necessary show them the bills. But don't labour it and don't make them feel guilty.

Educational Matters

Your child's education is your responsibility until the

age of 16, though this can continue to the age of 19.

Choosing schools can be a difficult task if you have several to choose from or if the nearest is one you don't like. Ideally, you should visit each school under consideration both unannounced and by appointment. Have a list of questions to ask and things to look out for.

✿ Get a feel of the atmosphere - is it friendly, are the children happy and hard-working, are you welcomed, is it noisy?

✿ Look for evidence of structured learning - displays on the wall (are they fresh?), reading, language and mathematics schemes, equipment for science, art, music, computers, sports etc

✿ Talk to the head teacher, to other staff and to parents of children already at the school. Does the ethos of the school encourage the development of learning, exploration, responsibility, respect and dignity?

Choosing subjects during secondary school can have far reaching effects on what your child does or does not end up doing in later life. There is no point pushing your child into hated subjects he/she is useless at. On the other hand, it is important to try and find a balance - English and Maths or a science are always worth pursuing alongside the more practical subjects such as domestic science or drama.

Listen to your child's point a view and discuss the pros and cons of their intended choices. In the end, go along with what they decide to do and give them your full support.

When it comes to choosing an A level or university course, you have to weigh up the pros and cons of vocational subjects or ones that are enjoyed. Very few vocational courses lead straight into a job these days - you usually have to take a vocational course on top of your degree.

The Disabled Member of the Family

Disabled people whether child or adult should always be made to feel part of the family. To do this involve them in all your activities and decisions, take them with you into the community and never make them feel isolated.

Caring for a disabled person can be very exhausting on you all but there is a lot of assistance available if you know where to look. Your local CAB or Social Services should be able to help and they will also be able to advise you on extra benefits the disabled person or you as carer can apply for.

Growing Up

Although children are the responsibility of their parents for most things until the age of 18 is reached, there are a number of legal restrictions on many activities.

What can you do, what can't you do legally and at what age? Some of the more common activities are listed below.

✪ At any age: smoke in private (but not buy cigarettes until you are 16); baby-sit, whether paid or not (it is the parents of the child who are responsible for matters of safety); take part in films, plays etc or do 'odd jobs' for relatives or neighbours

✪ At 5: drink alcohol in private (but not in a pub until you are 18)

✪ At 13: work, but not for more than 2 hours on Sundays or school days

✪ At 15: be sentenced to a prison sentence; open a Post Office giro account

☼ At 16: drive a moped; get a passport; leave school and work full time; receive confidential medical advice; get married with parental consent; change your name by deed poll; claim Income Support (eg if no longer a dependent) or Youth Training allowance; buy cigarettes, premium bonds, lottery tickets, fireworks

☼ At 17: drive most vehicles; buy a firearm or ammunition

☼ At 18: almost anything an adult is entitled to do (exceptions include standing at an election or selling alcohol)

Even though these are the legalities, this does not mean you can abdicate your responsibilities. If a controversial issue comes up, it is always best to discuss it and put across your point of view. Don't be afraid to put your foot down if you completely disagree. For example, you don't have to let your child smoke or drink in your house whatever their age.

12

Enjoying Your Family

I hope you haven't got the wrong idea by the time you reach this chapter. Families are not only about bringing children up the right way or getting on with grumpy grandma. At the end of the day, families are to be enjoyed.

One of the joys of bringing up a family is watching your children grow, change and mature. They quickly move from being toddlers to technological whizkids and before you know it they've left home to start up a new career at the other end of the country. So enjoy and treasure every moment while you can.

The art of enjoying your family is to imagine you are a ship at anchor riding out a storm - you survive and come through it by not resisting the ups and downs, the surges of anger and the quiet lulls in between. For the moment you start to fight the way things are blowing, that's when your troubles will begin. For instance, if your twelve year old daughter decides to become a vegetarian for whatever reason, you are going to have to accept it by providing non-meat alternatives. Insisting she eat the same meat as the rest of the family will only result in her digging in her heels more firmly and every meal time will become a battlefield.

Right from the start, you should make up your mind to provide a variety of activities you can all enjoy together. What you choose to do will vary from year to year as your children grow up and their tastes change. Following is a far from exhaustive list of some ideas to try out.

General activities for all families

Water Games

From the very first days, children enjoy playing in and with water. And if you're honest with yourself, so do you given half a chance. It begins with squeezing and sucking sponges and flannels in the bath and gradually develops into a life-long enjoyment of paddling and splashing in the shallows at the seaside or wallowing in a jacuzzi.

Water is a wonderful source of play (apart from having the slight disadvantage of being wet!) but one that is probably best reserved for outside the house or at the swimming pool. An old bathtub or inflatable paddling pool is your main requirement and during the warmer months it can almost be left out all the time. Provide an assortment of plastic ducks, boats and squeegy bottles, add water and away you go.

Although the children can be left to play alone it's

always a good idea to keep half an eye on what's going on, especially if there are toddlers about. But don't let them have all the fun - get out there and join in. Make sure everyone is suitably dressed to be completely saturated, arm everyone with a water pistol or squeegy bottle and you're ready for a gigantic splash-in! As adult in charge it will be up to you to make sure no-one gets over-excited; ideally you should set a strict time limit and then stop.

Family outings to the local swimming pool are a must. With any luck your pool will have special times for parents and babies/toddlers as well as organised fun sessions for older children.

In summer, make sure the whole family has at least one day at a seaside resort with clean, sandy beaches. You can combine paddling and splashing in the shallows with digging, burying and sand castle building in the sand.

The Great Outdoors - trips and activities out of the house

Wherever you live - town, city or village - there will be places to take the family. The nearest Tourist Information Bureau or library is likely to have a whole range of ideas on places to visit.

✿ Virtually every town has at least one area of parkland or woodland. Find out what's near you and make a point of visiting it regularly throughout the year. Just an hour strolling round it observing the changes in the seasons reflected in the trees and flowers is all it needs. And if you're lucky you'll have several recreation grounds and country parks to choose from. The local Parks Department will have a list of picnic areas you can visit

✿ Further afield, look out for natural features to visit such as a woodland lake, craggy outcrop or riverside walk. Many of these will be clearly waymarked for walkers and these will give you a chance to see nature closely

☼ Keep your eyes open for special family open days. Many large estates, agricultural colleges, farms, fire stations and country houses open their doors to the public on one or two weekends in a year. Because they are also likely to put on special events, games and refreshments at the same time, they can make a marvellous day out which are also that little bit unusual. Agricultural shows, country fairs, street markets and historical re-enactments are also a good source for a family day out. Go as a family to the theatre, cinema, music concert, ceilidh or sporting event

☼ Join your local sports or leisure centre and make use of their facilities and courses. Like swimming pools, you will find sessions regularly put on for families with special activities and opportunities to try out new sports or learn new skills

☼ Join the local branch of the Youth Hostels Association or Ramblers Association. You will find lots of organised activities, walks and weekends away that are ideal for all ages. Most YHA hostels now have family rooms and some even have self-contained family units

☼ Organise your own night walk for the family and your friends. It could end up with a barbecue. Make sure you are properly kitted out with torches, reflective clothing, proper footwear etc and only go if the weather is suitable. If possible, aim for a hill so that you can look at the lights below or watch the stars above. If you're quiet enough you may even see some nocturnal animal life

☼ Get involved in a local club or society that caters for all ages. Scout or Guide groups, for example, always welcome parental involvement. The amateur dramatics society will need people of all ages to act, help with costumes and scenery or assist with backstage work

Indoor Activities for when you want to stay at home

Thanks to our variable climate, much of our leisure time is going to be restricted to inside the house. The danger here is that the only thing anyone does together is watch the television, play video games or sit at the computer. Now all these pieces of technology are fine in themselves but they can take over the house if you're not careful. Over-dependence on them for entertainment will stifle conversation and shared activities will all but disappear.

You will therefore need a strict though flexible policy to restrict the amount of time spent sitting in front of a screen of one sort or another (and this includes any that may be lurking in the children's bedrooms). Rather than banning it completely, ration the amount of time each child can spend watching television etc and keep to it. The big advantage here is that it teaches the children to discriminate between programmes and hopefully will lead to them being able to make informed choices in the future.

There's no point rationing television if you're not going to make sure there is plenty for the family to do when the set is switched off. Here are some ideas that you can try out:

- ✿ Jigsaws left out on a board, table or roll-up mat can encourage everyone to work together to complete them
- ✿ Build up a collection of board games from *Twister* to *Monopoly*
- ✿ Buy a book of DIY games that include ideas for word games, charades and party fun
- ✿ Collect an assortment of construction toys such as Lego, train sets or Scalextric that everyone can join in with on the floor
- ✿ Keep one or two small pets such as gerbils, hamsters, fish or birds. Encourage the children to take it in turns to clean out the cages etc. Owning a dog is a good incentive to go on walks or to play with as a family
- ✿ In the autumn, design and make your own Christmas cards, decorations, crackers and gifts
- ✿ Make a family video with the camcorder. Perhaps you can go a step further and plan a script with the family as the cast

✿ Develop a love for books. Despite what computer/television advocates might say, you cannot substitute for the pleasure books can give you. They can be taken anywhere; you only have to read the bits you want to read; they will not cause a nuisance to anyone else (unless you leave them lying around everywhere); they are a great source of information, stories, poetry etc and a wonderful stimulus for the imagination. You don't have to buy them, you can borrow them from the library

✿ Sit together and tell each other stories. The children can be encouraged to retell stories heard at school or teach everyone songs they have learnt in the music lesson. Be prepared to make some sort of contribution yourself. Some commercial games such as 'Hullabaloo' and 'Pictionary' encourage you to get used to joining in through charades

✿ Have joke-telling sessions with everyone contributing. Encourage punning and play on words

✿ Organise parties for families. These can be held in the afternoon or early evening and two or three whole families can be invited. Plan a few games and activities. Fancy Dress or theme parties are also a way of increasing the potential for fun. For example, toddlers and younger children will enjoy lollipop or teddy bear picnic parties; older children might like a clown party in which everyone is face-painted, a balloon sports party or barbecue. Teenagers, on the other hand, may be attracted to a pyjama supper party in which their friends sleep over or, if you can bear the noise, a disco party

✿ Good times for family gatherings are Midsummer, Hallowe'en, Guy Fawkes, Christmas/New Year, Mother's Day and Easter. If you space them out throughout the year, it will give you all a regular event to look forward to and to plan for. It may also help you take the focus away from trivial bickering and feelings of boredom

A positive outlook

The key to enjoying your family to the full is to develop a positive attitude:

✷ Positive listening will show you are interested in what your children or partner are telling you. Don't rush them, don't keep interrupting and take your time to hear them out

✷ Positive talking will be honest, tactful and constructive. Be careful to choose the right words - ones that don't threaten, insult, punish or blame. Cut out negative statements wherever possible and when you do have to use them, qualify them with something positive

✷ A positive voice will be cheerful, caring and tender. Your tone will be low and affectionate

✷ Develop a positive body language. Smile, look sympathetic, adopt a good eye contact (but don't stare!), remain still and calm, lean forwards and, if appropriate, get physically close

✷ Involve the whole family in all decision making, especially when they will be affected by the decision. Even when a decision has been taken, take the time to explain why. Sharing decision-making can reduce the pressure and remove any possibilities of guilt or blame being cast if it subsequently goes wrong

Areas where decision-making needs to be shared by the family include: which TV programmes to watch, matters of diet and food, how leisure time is spent, pocket money, bedtimes and holidays. Your aim is to reach a sensible decision rather than one that tries to be 'fair' to everyone.

Lighting Your Way
to a Golden Future

Making contact - How to do it

Please note: all telephone helplines are listed separately in section ii - look out for the helpline symbol #.

Although the aim of this book is to enable you to take control of the action, there are going to be times when you will want to ask someone for help. There are hundreds of organisations and agencies across the country that are there specifically to give you that help. And in most cases, the help will be free. You should find that the advice you ask for will be given with impartiality and in confidence.

When you decide you need some extra help, it's important to be clear in your mind what you want to ask. When you have several problems you need help with, list them on a piece of paper so that you don't forget any of them. Then, all you have to do is find out when, where and how you make contact. Usually a telephone call will tell you the opening times for drop-in sessions or enable you to make an appointment.

Remember the following points:

✪   Advice agencies and help-lines are there for you to use

✪ You can expect to have your problems dealt with in confidence and with impartiality
✪ When writing off for information, include a stamped self-addressed envelope for the reply. This will always be appreciated especially by charitable organisations. Be clear in what you are asking for and to whom it should be sent
✪ Always be polite even when you're angry or upset. You're more likely to achieve a positive result when you are

The Citizens Advice Bureau

Free, independent, confidential and impartial advice given at over 700 bureaux across the country. Each one is linked to a continually updated information network on general aspects of benefits, employment, debt, care in the community, housing, health and many other subjects. If they don't have the answer, they can probably tell you who has. Look in the telephone book for the address and phone number of the nearest to you. The National Association of CABx has a general enquiry line: **0181 459 2780**. In Scotland, the number to ring is **0131 667 0156**.

Many national organisations have local or regional offices and these are the ones you should aim to contact first. Look in the telephone directory or ask at the library, information centre or Citizens Advice Bureau for the address of your nearest office. For reasons of confidentiality, it's not generally a good idea to send personal information by fax unless you are specifically asked to use this method.

Please note that, whereas most of the organisations listed provide free help and support, not all of them do. Make sure you check when making your initial contact.

i) Addresses

(No telephone numbers listed here are helplines)

General advice for families

✿ **Family Welfare Association** (FWA)
Helps families and individuals overcome the effects of poverty through trust funds, grants and practical or financial support. 501-505 Kingsland Road, London E8 4AU
Tel **0171 254 6251**

✿ **Family Crisis Line** #
Confidential phone helpline for people experiencing any type of domestic crisis. C/o Ashwood House, Ashwood Road, Woking GU22 7JW Tel **01483 722 533**

✿ **Family Holiday Association**
It provides holiday grants for deprived families. Hertford Lodge, East End Road, London N3 3QE Tel **0181 349 4044**

✿ **Home-Start UK**
It provides support, friendship and practical help for families with children under five, as well as training and guidance for local groups. 2 Salisbury Road, Leicester LE1 7QR
Tel **0116 233 9955**

✿ **Mothers' Union**
Worldwide organisation with many local branches aimed at promoting Christian family life. Mary Sumner House, 24 Tufton Street, London SW1P 3RB Tel **0171 222 5533**

✿ **National NEWPIN**
Parenting skills training programmes, counselling, befriending and general support are some of the services provided. It aims to promote relationships founded on respect, empathy and support. Sutherland House, 35 Sutherland Square, London SE17 3EE Tel **0171 703 6326**

✿ **Parentline** #
A network of local groups and drop-in centres. Telephone

helpline. Endway House, The Endway, Hadleigh, Essex SS7 2AN.

✩ **Parents at Work #**
Information and advice about childcare provision for working parents. Telephone helpline. 77 Holloway Road, London N7 8JZ Tel **0171 700 5772**

✩ **Play for Life Network**
Promotes and shares ideas for play activities that will help your children's social and emotional development. Runs local groups and quarterly magazine. 14 Glebe Road, Reading, Berks RG2 7AG Tel **01734 871281**

✩ **Pre-School Learning Alliance #**
Promotes playgroups for under-fives. Childcare telephone helpline. 69 Kings Cross Road, London WC1X 9LL.

One Parent / Step Families

✩ **Gingerbread** for one parent families - it provides help through local support groups and through nationally produced information publications. 35 Wellington Street, London WC2E 7BN. Tel **0171 240 0953**

In Northern Ireland: 169 University Street, Belfast BT7 1HR Tel **01232 231417**

In Scotland: Maryhill Community Centre, 304 Maryhill Road, Glasgow G20 7YE. Tel **0141 353 0989**

✩ **The National Council for One Parent Families**
It produces information on a range of subjects including the free booklet *Holidays for one-parent families*. 255 Kentish Town Road, London NW5 2LX Tel **0171 267 1361**

✩ **The Scottish Council for Single Parents**
13 Gayfield Square, Edinburgh EH1 3NX.
Tel **0131 556 3899**

✩ **HELP**
Holiday Endeavour for Lone Parents provides low-cost holidays for one parent families. C/o 52 Chequer Avenue, Hyde Park, Doncaster DN4 5AS Tel **01302 365139**

☼ **HOP**
Holidays One-Parents - low-cost holidays and discounted travel. 51 Hampshire Road, Droylsden, Manchester M43 7PH. Tel **0161 370 0337**

☼ **Stepfamily#**
The National Stepfamily Association - provides support, advice and information. Telephone helpline. Counselling service: Chapel House, 18 Hatton Place, London EC1N 8RU.
Tel **0171 209 2460**

Gay and Lesbian Parents

☼ **Happy Families**
It offers nationwide support and advice to lesbian, gay and bisexual parents and their children. PO Box 1060, Doncaster DN6 9QU. Tel **01302 702 601**

☼ **Parents Friend**
Counselling and support to parents, relatives and friends of gay people. C/o Voluntary Action Leeds, Stringer House, 34 Lupton Street, Leeds LS10 2QW. Tel **0113 2674627**

Crises - Abuse, violence, prison, phobias - also see helplines

☼ **Help & Advice Line for Offenders' Wives** (HALOW)
Advice and practical support to any relatives of men in prison. (Most of the larger prisons also have their own support groups). Summerfield Foundation, 260 Dudley Road, Winson Green, Birmingham B18 4HL. Tel **0121 454 3615**

☼ **Lifeline#**
Counselling for victims of violence in the home, incest or sexual abuse. Self-help groups, correspondence support, telephone helpline. The Old Bakehouse, Main Road, Hulland Ward, Ashbourne, Derby DE6 3EA

- ✿ **NO PANIC** (National Association for Phobias, Anxiety Neurosis Information & Care) #
  Provides support to both sufferers and their families. Telephone helpline. 93 Brands Farm Way, Randley, Telford TF3 2JQ
- ✿ **Prisoners Families Advice & Information Network (PAIN)**
  Advice and support regarding any aspect of prisoners and their families. Will make referrals and put you in touch with other related organisations. BM Pain, London WC1N 3XX. Tel **0181 542 3744**
- ✿ **Women's Aid Federation** #
  Advice, information and temporary refuge for women and their children when threatened by domestic violence. Telephone helpline. PO Box 391, Bristol BS99 7WS

Bereavement

- ✿ **Compassionate Friends** #
  It offers friendship and support to newly bereaved parents and their families. Telephone helpline. 53 North Street, Bristol BS3 1EN
- ✿ **CRUSE** #
  Breavement Care: Nearly 200 local branches offering free counselling, support and advice to all bereaved people. Bereavement helpline. Cruse House, 126 Sheen Road, Richmond, Surrey TW9 1UR. Tel **0181 940 4818**
- ✿ **Rainbow Centre**
  For children with cancer and life-threatening illness. A range of emotional support is provided for the whole family during the crisis period. Techniques range from counselling and art therapy to relaxation and massage. PO Box 604, Bristol BS99 1SW. Tel **0117 985 3343**

Divorce and Separation

✿ **Divorce Mediation and Counselling Service**
Aimed at helping parents reach amicable, realistic arrangements for the joint care of children before, during or after separation or divorce. 38 Ebury Street, London SW1W 0LU.
Tel **0171 730 2422**

✿ **Families Need Fathers** (FNF) #
Primarily aimed at eliminating unnecessary legal conflict by giving help and advice to men and women with access and custody problems. Information helpline. 134 Curtain Road, London EC2A 3AR. Tel **0171 613 5060**

✿ **National Family Mediation**
Mainly child related problems. There is usually a fee.
9 Tavistock Place, London WC1H 9SN. Tel **0171 383 5993**

✿ **Relate**
National Marriage Guidance. Over a hundred local branches providing counselling on relationship problems and family education. Over 130 local branches. Could be a fee.
Herbert Gray College, Little Church Street, Rugby CV21 3AP
Tel **01788 573 241**

Grandparents

✿ **Children Need Grandparents** (CNG)
Advice to grandparents who are refused access to their grandchildren. Send SAE. 2 Surrey Way, Laindon West, Basildon, Essex SS15 6PS Tel **01268 456929**

Activities

✿ **Youth Hostels Association**
Although the overnight prices are weighted in favour of young people, many hostels cater for the family with special family annexes and rooms.

England/Wales: Trevelyan House, 8 St Stephen's Hill, St Albans AL1 2DY. Tel **01727 855 215** Fax **01727 844 126**
Northern Ireland: Bradbury Buildings, 56 Bradbury Place, Belfast BT7 1RU Tel **01232 324 733**
Scotland: 7 Glebe Crescent, Stirling FK8 2JA Tel **01786 451181**

✿ **The Ramblers**
Local groups, quarterly magazine, discounts.
1-5 Wandsworth Road, London SW8 2XX
Tel **0171 582 6878**

ii) Telephone Helplines

These telephone lines are there for you to use when you need help of any kind.

✿ **Alcoholics Anonymous** 0171 352 3001
✿ **Childcare** 0171 837 5513 (Pre-School Learning Alliance helpline)
✿ **Childline** 0800 1111 (for children in danger/under stress)
✿ **Compassionate Friends** 0117 953 9639 (family bereavement)
✿ **Cruse** (bereavement) 0181 332 7227
✿ **Families Need Fathers** 0181 886 0970 (information line)
✿ **Lifeline** 01335 370825 (help for victims of violence/abuse)
✿ **Narcotics Anonymous** 0171 498 9005
✿ **NO PANIC** 01952 590545 (phobias, anxiety problems)
✿ **Parentline** 01702 559900 (parents under stress)
✿ **Parents at Work** 0171 700 5771 (Tues, Thurs, Fri)
✿ **Samaritans** 0345 909090 (or see local phone book)
✿ **StepFamily** 0990 168 388 (2-5pm/7-10pm weekdays)
✿ **Victims** (of crime) 0171 729 1252
✿ **Women's Aid** 0117 963 3542 (women in danger of domestic violence)

iii) Useful Publications

✿ The Need2Know series includes many relevant titles - *Help Yourself to a Job* by Jackie Lewis, *Breaking Up - Live your new life to the full* by Chris West, *Take a Career Break - Bringing up children without giving up your future* by Astrid Stevens, *Superwoman* - a guide for working mothers and *Travel Without Tears* - a guide for family holidays (both by Marion Jayawardene).

✿ The *Overcoming Common Problems* series published by Sheldon Press (SPCK) also includes many useful titles. These include: *Divorce and Separation* by Angela Willans, *Enjoying Motherhood* by Dr Bruce Pitt, *How to Bring up your Child Successfully* and *Making Marriage Work* by Dr Paul Hauck, *One Parent Families* by Diana Davenport and *A Step-Parent's Handbook* by Kate Raphael.

Bereavement

✿ **Help in Your Bereavement**
Christopher Herbert (Collins)
✿ **Helping Children Cope With Grief**
Rosemary Wells (Sheldon)
✿ **A Grief Observed**
C.S. Lewis (Fontana)
✿ **Coping With Bereavement**
Julie Armstrong-Colton (Need2Know)

Child Development

There are many useful guides on the market and the best idea is to browse through them for one you like. Two books by Penelope Leach (Penguin) can be particularly recommended:

✪ **Baby & Child**
A comprehensive guide dealing with the first five years of life
✪ **The Parents' A to Z**
An encyclopaedia of information for parents of any age group

Relationships

✪ Fiction is an extremely good route into exploring relationships and the following authors and titles are particularly readable: Lesley Glaister (*Trick or Treat* and *Honour Thy Father*); Eva Hanagan (*Holding On*); John Irving (*Hotel New Hampshire*); Deborah Moggach (*Stolen*); William Wharton (*Dad* and *Pride*); Henry Williamson (*The Beautiful Days*).

Teenagers/young people

✪ **Parenting Teenagers** Polly Bird (Need2Know)
✪ **Living With a Teenager** Suzy Hayman(Piatkus)
✪ **It's More Than Sex: A Survival Guide to the Teenage Years** Suzie Hayman (Wildwood House)
✪ **Parties for Older Children**
Angela Hollest/Penelope Gaine (Piatkus)

Activities for children

✪ **Printforce Ltd**
Has a large catalogue of affordable activity books *eg Fun for all Seasons* edited by Jean Barrow, 6 Angel Hill Drive, Sutton, Surrey, SM1 3BX Tel **0181 770 2090**

✿ **Come to a Party**
Delphine Evans (Hutchinson)

Index

INDEX

Also Published by

Need2Know

Parenting Teenagers

Make the Most of this Unique Relationship

Polly Bird
ISBN 1 86144-018-9
£5.99 100pp Pub Sep 96

Parenting Teenagers is the answer to all parents' prayers - a comprehensive guide to helping make the 'teenagers years' in any household as pleasurable as possible.

Packed with information, advice and tips, *Parenting Teenagers* is aimed at anyone who has the task of bringing up teenagers - parents and carers. It will also be of interest to those who work with teenagers such as teachers, social workers, youth leaders and so on.

Safe as Houses

Security and Safety in the Home

Gordon Wells
ISBN 1 86144-013-8
£5.99 100pp Pub July 96

650,000 burglaries take place in the UK each year; this is an average of 1 in every 49 seconds.

5,000 fatal accidents occur in the home in the UK every year.

With these statistics, everyone should be aware of the dangers and do everything possible to increase security and safety in the home.

Need2Know Series

For further details and to order further copies, please contact

Kerrie Pateman (Editorial)
Pat Wilson (Marketing)
Need2Know
1-2 Wainman Road
Woodston
Peterborough
Cambs
PE2 7BU

Tel 01733 390801
Fax 01733 230751

Need2Know are always interested in proposals for new titles.
Please contact the above address for information and brief.

Order Information

All Need2Know titles can be ordered through your local bookshop or direct from the publisher.

Payment Details

Please make cheques or postal orders payable to *Forward Press Ltd* adding £1 for postage and packing (if you are ordering more than three copies, postage and packing is free).

Please send orders to:

Distribution, Forward Press Ltd, 1-2 Wainman Road, Woodston, Peterborough PE2 7BU Tel: 01733 238140 Fax: 01733 230751

If you have any order queries please contact the above address.